The
Low-Carbohydrate
Gourmet

The Low-Carbohydrate Gourmet

A COOKBOOK FOR HUNGRY DIETERS

by Harriet Brownlee

William Morrow & Company, Inc.
New York 1975

Copyright © 1974 by Harriet Brownlee

Grateful acknowledgment is made to reprint recipes as follows:

Recipes for Poached Eggs Nimes, Chicken Beauvais, and Chicken Roquefort from THE WHITE HOUSE CHEF COOKBOOK by Rene Verdon, copyright © 1967 by Rene Verdon. Used by permission of Doubleday & Company, Inc.

Recipes for Fillet of Sole in White Wine and Fillet of Beef in Vermouth from THE PLEASURES OF ITALIAN COOKING by Romeo Salta, copyright © 1962 by Romeo Salta. Used by permission of Macmillan Publishing Co., Inc.

Recipes for Grilled Tidbit and Steak Moutarde Flambé from A TREASURY OF GREAT RECIPES by Mary & Vincent Price, copyright © 1965 by Mary & Vincent Price. Used by permission of Bernard Geis Associates, Inc.

Recipe for Steak with Mushroom Sauce from ANNEMARIE'S PERSONAL COOKBOOK by Annemarie Huste, copyright © 1968 by Annemarie Huste. Used by permission of The Foley Agency.

Printed in the United States of America.

1 2 3 4 5 78 77 76 75 74

Book design by Helen Roberts

Library of Congress Cataloging in Publication Data

Brownlee, Harriet.
    The low-carbohydrate gourmet.

    1. Low-carbohydrate diet. I. Title.
RM237.9.B76   641.5′634   74-14657
ISBN 0-688-02874-8

To all adults who were once fat children, and now, through no fault of their own, must diet for the rest of their lives.

Foreword

The excessive eating of carbohydrate foods (sugars and starches) seems to be the current "fat culprit" on the dietary horizon. In my opinion, any dietary regime offering a satisfying approach to the control of carbohydrate intake is not only a welcome addition to the vast numbers of theories on weight control, but also a sensible approach to good nutrition.

Harriet Brownlee, in THE LOW-CARBOHYDRATE GOURMET, offers painlessly sound and sensible methods for low-carbohydrate cooking and eating. She wisely suggests that even with carbohydrate control, food intake should be both reasonably limited and nutritionally safe. Along with her sound advice for subsidizing a low-carbohydrate diet with vitamins and minerals as well as a doctor's supervision, she also provides myriad suggestions for satisfying an addictive "sweet tooth" and for preparing other "unheard-of-on-a-diet" foods with the use of low-carbohydrate substitutes.

Ms. Brownlee discusses the danger of the over-enthusiastic claims of most other diets and the possible pitfalls of unsound nutrition even in carefully controlled dietary regimes. She shows how dieters need not resort to fad gimmicks, fad foods, fad recipes—fad diets—in order to lose weight or to maintain one's desired weight.

As a result of her own personal experience in her fight with fatness, she has created a cookbook for dieters which works both to insure weight loss and to prevent dieting from being a chore or a bore. This book, a needed companion for all those (30 million plus!) in the frequently lonesome world of dieters, is sometimes solemnly, sometimes amusingly, always sensibly written. It is truly a gourmet cookbook—especially for dieters!

ABRAHAM WEINBERG, M.D.

Acknowledgments

No book is ever solely the work of one person. Many people have influenced me in the writing of this book and I would like to take this opportunity to give them my thanks:

First to my mother for encouraging my interest in cooking from childhood and for being my extra pair of hands in recent years during the writing of the book; to Dr. Arnold Zentner for giving me the freedom to create; to Mrs. Shirley Shure for originally teaching me to bake; to Dr. Robert C. Atkins for stimulating and fostering my interest in low-carbohydrate cooking; to Dr. Ivor Schapiro for his gentle encouragement and support throughout the writing of the book; to John Schaffner and Victor Chapin for their faith in me when no one wanted to give a beginner a chance; to Miss Barbara Chafetz for her assistance in typing the manuscript.

Contents

Preface

One of my dreams has always been that medical science would find the way to make me burn all of my food normally and that I would never have to diet again. How many of you have shared that dream with me? To suddenly be able to eat anything you want and not to gain even one pound! Imagine being able to eat without getting fat!

Fat! How I hate that word! I'm sure it is one of the ugliest words in the English language. It even sounds ugly! I think I would rather starve to death than ever to allow myself to get fat. Some of you will hate me instantly when you read this, but I am five feet, five inches tall and weigh 120 pounds. I can hear you saying already, "How can she write a diet cookbook? How can anyone who's that thin understand what it's like to be fat and have to diet? She's not one of us."

Yes, I am thin. I've been thin all of my adult life. But let me share some of my childhood memories with you. I remember when I was twelve years old and my eighth grade teacher weighed and measured the class and called out the figures for everyone to hear: Harriet Brownlee, 5'0" tall, 170 pounds. My classmates snickered and laughed at me and how I wished I could hide under my desk or that the floor would open up and I could crawl under it! I pray that teachers don't do that anymore! I remember trying to learn to ride a bicycle and to roller skate, but being too embarrassed because I was so awkward and so clumsy. I never did learn to do either. I remember when my mother would take me shopping for clothes. "We have nothing here that could possibly fit her. She's too fat. Try another store."

"No, we have nothing that she could wear here. Why don't you lose weight, dear? You'd be so pretty if you did. Try the Chubbie Department. Maybe they'll have something." I remember how we bought two identical skirts one year, just in different colors. They were the only ones we could get that fit me and my mother was getting disgusted by that time. Were they size 44 or 46? I can't remember, but does it really matter which? I remember graduating from the eighth grade. My mother had to have my graduation dress made for me. It was white organdy. We couldn't find a white dress to fit me in any store. I was the smartest girl in my graduating class. I even had the highest I.Q., but I only remember the sensitive little girl looking out of the window on graduation night with the tears streaming down her face, trying to hide the tears from her family. I was the only pupil in my whole graduating class who didn't get invited to any of the graduation parties, the only one who was completely left out.

I've worn a lot of beautiful designer clothing since those years. I'm a size eight now. Even though I never learned to roller skate or to ride a bicycle, in college I learned to swim so gracefully that everyone stops to watch me. And there have been many parties since then, too—parties where I have been the most beautiful young woman in the room. But those childhood memories will be recorded in my mind forever, and even as I wrote about them, the tears were streaming down my face.

This book is my gift to the diet world. The recipes I have included have enabled me to stay on one of the strictest versions of a low-carbohydrate diet for over four years—and thus to maintain my normal weight. These recipes were originally developed for me because I missed sweets so much. Without them, I doubt that I could have continued such a diet faithfully for such a long time.

I am proud to be able to share my book with you. To give a gift is to give a part of oneself, but for a gift to be valuable, it must be used, not just stored away in a closet. Don't just read the recipes and say, "Umm, that sounds delicious." (And they *are* delicious!) Use these recipes and let them make and keep you thin!

The
Low-Carbohydrate
Gourmet

Introduction

Yes, nobody likes to be fat. But at the same time, nobody, but nobody, likes to diet! We diet simply because we have to. There are those of us whom Fate has willed to be fat, but since fashion and good health dictate that we be thin, we have had to feel exempt from the human race at mealtimes. Worse yet, because diet food has, until now, been so unappetizing, often after we have succeeded in losing a few pounds we have gone back to fattening eating again. Up goes the scale; nobody can spend a lifetime feeling deprived.

Only by acquiring a new eating life-style can one *stay* thin. Anyone who has ever had a serious weight problem eventually knows he must "diet" in some way for the rest of his life, and until medical science discovers a fat-melting pill, dieting will remain the only answer. But how does one go about choosing a diet that allows one to either lose pounds or maintain a low weight, while at the same time allowing him not to feel deprived? Today, the choices of diets are innumerable:

A Complete Starvation Diet: This was the first diet I ever tried and I learned at the young age of 13 that the only thing this diet would do was make me sick. This isn't just a diet with *bad* nutrition—this one has *no* nutrition!

The Ten-Day Egg Diet or *The Mayo Clinic Diet:* This diet never originated in the Mayo Clinic! After trying it during my college years, I could never again stand the sight of a hard-cooked egg. I must admit that it did take some pounds off me in those ten days, but on the tenth day, I promptly passed out. This diet is not only poor nutritionally, it leaves you in a state of constant hunger.

The Old Blitz Diet: By eating cottage cheese and fruit three times a day, you are supposed to take off five pounds in two days. I lost ½ pound in four days and was gagging on the cottage cheese by the first night. I didn't mind cottage cheese and fruit for lunch, but for breakfast and dinner, too? Having to eat cottage cheese for dinner, especially on cold winter nights, made me feel inhuman. This diet is psychologically unsatisfying and is also poor nutritionally if you stay on it for any length of time.

The Old Calorie-Counting Diets: I lived with these diets for many years—until I learned better. They did work and even kept me thin. But in order to lose weight or even to maintain my weight, I had to keep my calorie intake so low that not only was I always hungry, I had the worst health of anyone I know. I had no resistance to disease, took three times as long as anyone else to heal when I got sick and was always weak and tired. I have iron will power and rarely break any diet, so I managed to live with low-calorie diets for years. However, I also severely aggravated a case of hypoglycemia—low blood sugar—by always walking around hungry, and came close to losing my life because of it. The damage done during those years can never completely be undone.

If you severely restrict calories all of your life, you cannot get enough basic nutrition to keep you healthy. Besides, most people who aren't as motivated to be thin usually give up when the hunger becomes unbearable.

The Diet Pill Way: Doctors hand these out much too freely! Every doctor I had ever been to up until a few years ago handed me prescriptions for diet pills when I complained I had trouble staying thin. They all assume that you're a glutton and eat too much. Diet pills actually are meant to make you lose weight by suppressing your appetite so that you will cut down your calories. But the minute you stop taking them, your appetite returns in full force. The only way you can stay thin with them is by continuing to take them. Apart from the damage they can do to your body, do you really want to be hooked? The last doctor who tried to hand me a prescription—and even some sample diet pills—had the sorry experience of having his prescription ripped up in front of his eyes and his samples thrown in his own wastebasket. I suggest you do the same to any doctor who tries to give them to you! His medical treatment deserves that kind of treatment from you!

Dr. Stillman's Quick-Weight-Loss Diet: I've known many people who have lost weight on this diet, but gained a great amount right back the minute they began to eat normally. Mainly, this diet does not teach good eating habits. Nobody can live on just meat, hard-cooked eggs, cottage cheese, and water for the rest of his life. Besides the fact that this is bad nutritionally (I faint on this diet and have known many others who either faint or feel very weak), this diet is boring.

Weight-Watchers Diet: If this diet works for you, use it by all means. It is nutritionally sound and can do you no harm. However, it will not necessarily do you any good either, because it does not work for everyone. I think you may have to be severely overweight to have this diet work for you. I gain weight on it, as do a number of others I've met. Besides, all that fish!

By this time, if you're starting to wonder if the only thing you can do is stay round, take heart. There is still one diet that I have not mentioned. Imagine a diet that lets you eat gourmet meals! Imagine a diet you will be able to stick to when eating in any restaurant! Imagine a diet that does not force you to eat any particular food you do not like! Imagine a diet that lets you have good wines with your dinner! Imagine a diet that lets you lose weight and keep it off forever with just a minimum of willpower! Imagine a diet that's fun!

No, this diet does not exist only in your dreams. It's a diet that you can start living with right now. It's a high-protein, low-carbohydrate diet.

There are many variations of the basic low-carbohydrate diet. The one factor they all have in common is that they all restrict carbohydrates but do not restrict calories—hence no hunger. Carbohydrate foods are those that contain high percentages of sugar (which is pure carbohydrate) and starch, including fruits, breads, cakes, candies, pies, soda containing sugar, puddings, cereal, pasta, and some vegetables such as corn and sweet potatoes. Meat, fish, poultry, eggs, butter, oil, margarine, and some mayonnaises contain no carbohydrates while cheeses and salad greens contain only a few.

It's a good idea when starting this diet to equip yourself with a carbohydrate gram-counting chart. (See the chart on page 240 of this book.) Comprehensive charts are available in any paperback book shop. An excellent reference is Barbara Kraus's *Calories and*

Carbohydrates°, which is now available in paperback. In addition, The Department of Agriculture Handbook Number Eight, *Composition of Foods*†, can be obtained inexpensively by writing to the Government Printing Office. *Dr. Carlton Fredericks' Low-Carbohydrate Diet* contains excellent lists, and even Adelle Davis's *Let's Eat Right to Keep Fit* contains a food-value listing you can look at, though it is not complete.

The most liberal of the low-carbohydrate diets is *The Drinking Man's Diet*, otherwise known as *The Air Force Diet*. To follow this diet, you may eat anything you want to as long as you limit yourself to less than 60 grams of carbohydrates per day. There are no limits placed on any other foods. If you lose weight easily, by all means follow this diet. It's the easiest of all.

Dr. Carlton Fredericks offers two different food plans for your low-carbohydrate diet. The easier of the two simply asks you to limit your carbohydrate intake to 60 grams per day, eat cheese and eggs in specified amounts, drink two glasses of milk per day, and eat six small meals a day instead of three larger ones. His stricter food plan places limits on everything.

I object to his insistence on the two glasses of milk. I do not feel that anyone, particularly a dieter whose food is restricted, should ever be forced to eat anything he doesn't like, and I know there are many people like myself who detest milk. Why not meet your minimum daily allowances with cheese? On days when I may not feel like eating cheese, I'm not above popping a few calcium pills into my mouth instead to meet my minimun daily requirement. On the other hand, his suggestion that you eat six small meals a day instead of the usual three large ones is excellent and has been recommended to dieters for years. In an article called "Meal Frequency—A Possible Factor in Human Pathology" in *The American Journal of Clinical Nutrition* (August, 1970), an experiment is described showing how both men and women, when fed small, frequent meals, were able to eat more than 1400 calories in excess of the normal intake they needed to maintain their normal weight, without gaining any weight.

° Barbara Kraus's *Calories and Carbohydrates* was originally published by Grosset and Dunlap, New York, in 1971. The paperback edition is published by New American Library, New York.

† To obtain *Composition of Foods*, write to the U.S. Government Printing Office, Washington, D. C. 20402. If you live in the New York area, this book can be obtained quickly by a short trip to the Government Printing Office, Federal Plaza, Foley Square, New York City. Phone 264-3826.

But when they were fed the same amount of food in two large meals, they did gain weight to the degree of their calorie excess.

A recent diet book, *Dr. Atkins' Diet Revolution,* aroused a storm of controversy. One of the biggest criticisms leveled at Dr. Atkins by the American Medical Association was that his diet was too high in saturated fats. I think one of the things that the A.M.A. failed to realize is that by natural selectivity people will vary their diet. Even if you are allowed to eat only eggs, beef, butter, etc., you will not necessarily take in too much. People want variety in their meals and practically everyone would get sick of eating steaks, roast beef, or very rich food every single day, let alone having to pay for them in these inflationary times.

I do feel that Dr. Atkins should place some restrictions on the *amounts* of food people eat. I'm not saying people should count every calorie, but they should be aware that they shouldn't eat even protein foods out of boredom or unhappiness, for amusement or sociability, or even just because it's mealtime. If you eat only in reasonable quantities, you will not eat an unreasonable amount of fat. And if your doctor advises you, because of your particular state of health, to restrict your intake of saturated fats, many high-protein, low-carbohydrate recipes can be just what you should be using so that you can follow his orders without also going on a dreary "I-can't-eat-anything" diet. As a general rule of thumb: The saturated fats people are usually told to avoid are found in butter, egg yolk, cream cheese and cheeses made from cream or whole milk, sweet or sour cream, beef, lamb, liver, and shrimp. Avoid these and concentrate on egg whites, cheeses made from skimmed or partially skimmed milk, fish other than shellfish, fowl, veal and soy flour. Substitute margarine or oil for butter, farmer's cheese for cream cheese, or whipped non-fat dry milk for cream. In any recipes where I combined heavy cream and water, substitute skimmed milk in the same proportion of liquid: ¼ cup cream plus ½ cup water equals ¾ cup skimmed milk, so use ¾ cup skimmed milk. You do raise the carbohydrate count, but the food will be good.

I've used Dr. Atkins' diet myself for the past four years and find it is the only diet that allows me to eat a normal amount of food without gaining weight. He devised an individual diet for me when I was his patient, and I have lived with the maintenance part of his diet since then. We found that carbohydrates are definitely what threw my weight out of line and that I could not tolerate more than 30 grams daily without gaining. But even with this strict limitation on carbohydrates, I cannot take in unlimited food without having unlimited inches show on my waistline. Probably no one can. However, without restricting carbohydrates, I used to have to live on six to seven hundred calories a day—not to lose weight, but just to maintain it.

The biggest advantage of the low-carbohydrate diet is that you can follow it forever and thus keep from ever again adding on excess pounds that you will have to strenuously diet away. The low carbohydrate diet is safe. John Yudkin, the English scientist, in his article "The Nutrient Intake of Subjects on a Low-Carbohydrate Diet Used in the Treatment of Obesity" in *The American Journal of Clinical Nutrition* (July, 1970), states that after 15 years of experience with this diet, none of his subjects complained of hunger and several stated an increased feeling of well-being and decreased lassitude. He concludes that the low-carbohydrate diet presents no health hazard, either generally or in regard to its nutritional value. The nutrient value is appreciably higher than could have been achieved had his subjects reduced their calorie intake to achieve the same degree of weight loss by an overall reduction in a normal diet.

My recipes are so low in carbohydrates that they can be used in any of the low-carbohydrate diets including the well-known ones previously mentioned: Dr. Carlton Fredericks' low-carbohydrate diet, The Air Force Diet, and Dr. Atkins' diet. With each recipe, I have provided the number of grams of carbohydrates for the entire recipe as well as for each serving. (For those who are also intent on keeping track of their calorie intake, I have included the total and per-serving calorie counts for each recipe. A number of books exist that will tell you what your maximum calorie intake should be according to your sex, age, height, etc. However, as I have said, calorie counting never really worked for me.) Find out the number of grams of carbohydrate per day your body requires to lose or to maintain weight, whichever you are trying to do. Most of the diets limit you to 60 grams per day in order to lose weight, though as I mentioned before, I've discovered that I can assimilate only 30. You may have to experiment a bit, as well as follow carefully any other directions that the diet you have chosen may be based on, such as eating six small meals, or eating a specified amount of cheese, or drinking a certain number of glasses of milk. Once you have found the gram count that is right for you, turn to the recipes in this book that most appeal to you, and enjoy yourself!

These recipes are designed to make an easy diet even easier —and much more fun, too. Until now, if you were on a low-carbohydrate diet, you had to accept the fact that even though you never had to bear the torture of walking around hungry all day while dieting, all the foods you enjoyed most were the ones you must permanently give up. You also had to accept the fact that once you reached the weight you desired, these things had to *remain* a part of the past or the pounds would creep right back up on you again. Gone were hot muffins for weekend breakfasts. Gone were cakes and ice cream for snacks and dessert. Gone was the potato salad and the bun for the hamburger. Gone, certainly, was anything chocolate. That is, gone until now!

Now, using the recipes I have collected and created, you can eat gourmet meals at home. (How does a dinner of Consommé with Sherry, Glazed Rock Cornish Hen, Tossed Salad Vinaigrette, and Chocolate Rum Cream Roll for dessert sound? The recipes are all in this book.) You can remain on your diet while eating out (with a minimum of study, you'll soon know how to choose foods carefully), and even enjoy a glass of wine. The chapter that is my greatest pride, "Yes, You Can Bake With Soy Flour," is made up of carefully tested recipes for foods you felt were gone forever: the muffins, pancakes, fancy cakes, and even things chocolate! Imagine good-tasting food that's good for you—both nutritionally and dietetically.

Just so you will get a first look at how scrumptious it is all going to be, and so you can begin planning low-carbohydrate menus of your own, I have compiled the following sample menus for breakfast, brunch, lunch, and dinner. Enjoy your new, thin life-style; enjoy the new, thin you!

SOME SAMPLE MENUS

Breakfast

1. Cheese and Herb Omelet
    Hot Coffee or Tea
2. Cheddar Scrambled Eggs
    Sausage
    Hot Coffee or Tea
3. Broiled Bacon Strips
    Easy-Mix Muffins with Butter and Sugarless Strawberry Jam
    Hot Coffee or Tea
4. Double-Cheese Omelet
    Cinnamon-Pecan Puffins
    Hot Coffee or Tea

Brunch

1. Fresh Strawberries with Cream
    My Favorite Omelet
    Easy-Mix Muffins
    Hot Coffee or Tea
2. Cantaloupe Wedges with Fresh Mint
    Ham-Mushroom Omelet
    Cinnamon-Pecan Puffins
    Hot Coffee or Tea
3. Mushroom Soufflé Omelet
    Broiled Bacon Strips
    Cinnamon Bread with Cream Cheese and Sugarless Jam
    Hot Coffee or Tea
4. Easy-Mix Pancakes with Butter and Sugarless Maple Syrup or
    Jam
    Sausage
    Hot Coffee or Tea
5. French Toast with Sugarless Maple Syrup or Jam
    Broiled Bacon Strips
    Hot Coffee or Tea
6. Cantaloupe Wedge

Ham Omelet
Cinnamon Bread with Nutted Cream Cheese
Hot Coffee or Tea

Lunch

1. Salade Niçoise
   Lemon Cake-Pudding
   Iced Coffee or Tea
2. Mushroom, Herb, and Cheese Omelet
   Tossed Lettuce and Tomato Salad with Oil, Vinegar, and Garlic
      Dressing
   Raspberry Sponge Pudding
3. Cheese-Filled Hamburgers
   Potato-like Salad
   Sugarless Soda
4. Curried Chicken Salad on a Bed of Lettuce
   Cantaloupe Wedges
   Iced or Hot Tea
5. French Omelet Filled with Chicken Liver Sauté
   Tossed Green Salad with Vinaigrette Dressing
   Easy-Mix Muffins with Butter (served hot)
   Chocolate Almond Pudding

Dinner

1. Cold Shrimp with Dilled Shrimp Sauce
   Consommé with Sherry
   Glazed Rock Cornish Hens
   Tossed Salad with Garlic-flavored Vinaigrette Dressing
   Chocolate Rum Cream Roll
   Hot Coffee or Tea
2. Cold Strawberry Soup
   Steak with Mushroom and Wine Sauce
   Green Beans Amandine
   Bibb Lettuce and Tomato Salad with Roquefort or Vinaigrette
      Dressing
   Lemon Cream Roll
   Coffee or Constant Comment Spiced Tea

3. Fresh Mushroom Soup (hot in winter or cold in summer)
    Broiled Chicken with Shallot Butter
    Tossed Green Salad with Roquefort Dressing
    Strawberry or Chocolate Ice Cream
    Hot or Iced Coffee or Tea

4. Hot Onion Soup
    Chicken Beauvais
    Green Beans Amandine
    Tossed Salad with Garlic-flavored Vinaigrette Dressing
    Lemon Chiffon Pie with a Brazil Nut Crust
    Hot Coffee or Tea

5. Greek Lemon Soup
    Lamb Shish Kebab
    Strawberry Ice Cream
    Hot Coffee

6. Melon with Prosciutto
    Beef Stroganoff
    Tossed Salad with Garlic-flavored Vinaigrette Dressing
    Assorted Dessert Cheeses
    Hot Coffee or Tea

7. Assorted Cold Hors d'Oeuvre
    Party Veal Scallops
    Braised Endive
    Lemon Mousse with Strawberries
    Hot Coffee or Tea

8. Cold Lemon Sorrel Soup
    Shad en Papillote
    Braised Celery
    Tomato Salad
    Chocolate Mousse
    Iced or Hot Coffee

9. Meat-Crusted Pizza
    Tossed Green Salad with Vinaigrette Dressing
    Vanilla or Chocolate Ice Cream
    Hot Coffee

10. Roast Chicken with Butter and Tarragon
    Cauliflower with Cheese
    Tossed Green Salad with Garlic-flavored Vinaigrette Dressing
    Jelly Roll with Apricot Jam Filling
    Hot Coffee or Tea

Tips for Low-Carbohydrate Cooks & Dieters

TIPS FOR COOKS

1.   Experiment with different blends of coffee. Jamaican Blue Mountain coffee is superb although expensive.

2.   Experiment with different types of teas to get flavor variations. You can now get teas from Mainland China that are delicious.

3.   Try French Gourmandise cheese with kirsch or walnuts, or French Rambol cheese covered with walnuts as a dessert when you have no time to make a diet dessert.

4.   Add extra sweetener to the artificially sweetened gelatins. It heightens the flavor.

5.   Concentrate on the following low-carbohydrate vegetables when planning your menus: Asparagus, mushrooms, spinach, cucumbers, green beans, celery, cauliflower, zucchini, endive, escarole, and peppers. These vegetables are also low in calories, and contain needed vitamins and minerals. Beware of high carbohydrate vegetables such as corn, peas, lima beans, beets and both white and sweet potatoes.

6.   The best low-carbohydrate buys in fruit are cantaloupe, honeydew melons, strawberries, apricots, peaches, rhubarb, tangerines and fresh pineapple. Beware of high carbohydrate fruits such as watermelon, cherries, bananas, apples and oranges.

7.   Beware of some cheeses, particularly processed cheeses and the so-called dietetic cheeses, because often they are high in carbohydrates. Some examples are Borden's process Neufchâtel, Wispride, Kraft natural primost and even my beloved Gjetost. Any of the natural cheeses mentioned in my recipes are safe.

8. Beware of most bottled salad dressings, including imitation mayonnaise, even the low-calorie and dietetic ones. There are fairly high in carbohydrates. Concentrate on the salad dressing recipes in this book, and, with regard to mayonnaise, I suggest Hellmann's. If you must use bottled dressings, those lower in carbohydrates include Slimette blue cheese, Green Goddess, and Tillie Lewis' Italian or Whipped dressings.

9. To save money, buy a roast of beef and have the butcher cut it into steaks. A whole fillet of beef is a good buy when it is on sale.

10. Liver and other organ meats may be high in iron, but they are also high in carbohydrates. Beware, also, of processed meats that are made with corn syrup.

11. Measure or weigh soy flour in a plastic bag. Add the baking powder and salt to the bag and then sift all dry ingredients directly into the liquid.

12. A kitchen scale is invaluable. Most kitchen scales give weight in both ounces and grams so you can have a precise idea of exactly how many grams of carbohydrates you will be consuming. Measuring by weight is the most accurate way to measure and is much easier than measuring with cups.

13. Get out of the kitchen if you are over-tired and rest for a little while. Otherwise, the only thing you will succeed in doing is having an accident or ruining something you are attempting to prepare. You may even find yourself nibbling unnecessarily!

SOME USEFUL INGREDIENTS FOR LOW-CARBOHYDRATE COOKING

Artificial Sweeteners

Artificial sweeteners are available in granulated, liquid and tablet forms. For many of the recipes in this book, granulated sweetener is a must. It is available from various companies, but be careful as some brands contain more carbohydrates than others. This must be taken into account when counting the carbohydrate gram content of a recipe. My favorite sweetener for my recipes is Sweet Magic made by the Cumberland Packing Company, because it has no carbohydrates at all. My second choice is Sweet'n Low, also made by the Cumberland Packing Company. By the time this book goes to press, cyclamate sweeteners will be returning. As soon as they are available, I suggest using them because they have a much better flavor.

A brown sugar substitute is also available under the name Brown Sugar Twin and it is quite good. I've used it in a few recipes in this book.

Cheeses

Swiss Gruyère Cheese. I have used imported Swiss Gruyère cheese in a number of recipes in this book. This is not the processed Gruyère like Swiss Knight or other wedged types, but is a cheese similar to Swiss Emmenthal with small holes and a nutty flavor. It's marvelous for cooking as well as for eating.

Parmesan Cheese. Buy imported Italian Parmesan cheese in a chunk and grate it freshly in your blender whenever you need it. Parmesan cheese may be stored in the freezer.

Ricotta Cheese. This is the Italian form of cottage cheese. It is unsalted and is used for Italian cheesecakes and Italian pastries such as Cannoli. Because it is smooth and delicious, I have used it as a filling for my cream roll cakes and to take the place of ice cream in milkshakes. It absorbs flavorings very well.

Farmer's Cheese. This is a pressed cottage cheese. The advantage of using Farmer's cheese rather than cottage cheese is that because the water has been pressed out, such dishes as cheesecake and blintzes are not too moist.

Chinese and Japanese Ingredients (Specialties)

Chinese Bean Curd. These little cakes of bean curd are made from soy beans and are an inexpensive source of protein. They absorb flavor well and are particularly suited to the taste of soy sauce. Use them in making Sukiyaki or cut them into cubes, dip them in soy sauce and use as a Chinese hors d'oeuvre.

Chinese Celery Cabbage. This vegetable is a cross between celery and cabbage. It is becoming increasingly popular and can now be found in fruit and vegetable stores and supermarkets as well as in Chinatown. Use it as a vegetable in Chinese stir-fried dishes or in a salad.

Chinese Dried Mushrooms. These marvelous thick, meaty mushrooms are only available in Chinese specialty shops, but are definitely worth seeking out. As a substitute, you can use Japanese dried mushrooms, but they are not as meaty. They will keep well without refrigeration in an airtight container. Use them in Chinese stir-fried dishes.

Chinese Five Spice Powder. This spice is available only in Chinese specialty shops. If you do not have access to one, combine equal parts of powdered cinnamon, powdered cloves, powdered aniseed and thyme. (Only 4 spices, but the taste is similar.) It is a delicious addition to Chinese Roast Pork.

Chinese Sesame Oil. This is available in any Oriental food shop, Japanese or Chinese, and is *not* the same as the sesame oil found in health food stores. Use it in Chinese-style salad dressings.

Rice Vinegar. Rice vinegar is used for Chinese and Japanese recipes. Kikkoman rice vinegar is excellent and is available in supermarkets. A trip to any Oriental food store will yield other appropriate brands.

Sake. This is a Japanese rice wine and is used in Japanese recipes. It is available in any liquor store. A dry sherry can be used as a substitute.

Soy Sauce. Buy imported soy sauce because the American soy sauce is far too salty. Chinese soy sauce is now coming into the United States from Mainland China and is absolutely delicious. Japanese Kikkoman soy sauce is also very good and is available in all supermarkets. Use it if the Chinese soy sauce is unavailable. See my recipe for Chinese Salad Dressing, page 196, for an interesting use for soy sauce.

Chives

Fresh chives are a delicious addition to eggs, cottage cheese, meats, and poultry, among other things. Chives are available frozen or dried, but fresh are the best and can be bought at good fruit and vegetable markets. Chop them, place them in an airtight plastic container, and freeze them yourself. If you have a sunny window, try growing them in little pots. They require very little attention since they are basically a weed.

Cornstarch

I've used very tiny amounts of cornstarch in my Chinese recipes, but one teaspoon of cornstarch contains 2.3 grams of carbohydrate. If you do not want to use these few extra grams, you may always eliminate the cornstarch.

Cream of Tartar

Unless you own a copper bowl for beating egg whites, always add ¼ teaspoon of cream of tartar for every two egg whites you beat. The cream of tartar adds the needed acidity that helps stabilize the egg whites so that they beat more easily and retain their firmness.

Curry Powder

Even if you've never liked curry before, try experimenting with various brands because each one has a different taste and you may find one that you like. My favorite is an imported Madras curry power produced under The Sun Brand label.

Dill

Fresh dill is available in all good fruit and vegetable markets. Dried dillweed can be obtained in jars, but fresh dill is far more delicious.

Eggs

Eggs are one of the best buys in protein. Buy the freshest eggs possible. Test an egg's freshness by immersing it in cold water. If it lies flat, it is very fresh; if it sits up, it is not fresh and should not be eaten. Anything in between may be used for baking, but I don't suggest using it for an egg dish. Store eggs in the refrigerator, then to bring to room temperature, immerse them in warm water for 5 to 10 minutes.

Extracts

Extracts are available in a wide variety of flavors. Different brands differ in taste, so experiment. Wagner's has an excellent selection including such flavors as chocolate, banana, raspberry, mocha, coconut, etc. Ehler's has good extracts also. If none of these is available near you, Insuperable Extract Company at 409 East 116th Street, New York, New York 10029, will gladly mail some to you. Just send for their catalog. Their selection is enormous and their extracts are the best quality of any I have seen. I buy their butter extract, which is excellent, in pint-sized bottles.

Food Coloring

Food coloring is available in all supermarkets. It is completely harmless and completely tasteless. Just follow the directions on the box for the color you desire.

Ginger Root & Ginger Juice

Fresh ginger root is available in Oriental or Spanish markets. In the fall, the young ginger comes into season and it, with its delicate flavor, is my favorite. Fresh ginger can be stored in dry sherry in an airtight container placed in the refrigerator. It will keep indefinitely. I have had success freezing it also, but I prefer it stored in sherry. Ginger juice is made by squeezing the fresh ginger root through a garlic press. The resulting ginger juice is excellent when used in Chinese stir-fried dishes or Chinese salad dressing.

Mayonnaise

Mayonnaise and salad dressing are not the same. Either you can make your own mayonnaise or buy Hellmann's on the East Coast or Best Foods on the West Coast. These contain the least sugar.

Mushrooms

Buy only firm, crisp, closed white mushrooms. When mushrooms are brown or open it means they have been sitting around too long. Mushrooms should not be washed. If they are closed, it will not be necessary. They should be wiped with a damp paper towel or damp cloth only. If you've never eaten raw mushrooms, by all means try them!

Oil

For salads, I like good quality olive oil. The Italian Bertolli, the French Old Monk or the French James Plagniol are all good. Health food stores carry a cold pressed garlic and oil which tastes good, too. Peanut oil is used for Chinese cooking and is available in any supermarket.

Pam

Pam is one of the latest marvels to come to the market shelves. Spray any pan with Pam and it will keep food from sticking, consequently allowing you to use less butter or oil in a recipe. It's particularly good for muffin pans, cake pans, etc.

Prosciutto

This is Italian smoked ham. It is customarily sliced into very thin slices and used in many Italian recipes or as an appetizer wrapped around cantaloupe wedges. If it is unavailable, a mild Westphalian ham may be substituted.

Shallots

Shallots are a cross between garlic and onions. They are used a great deal in French cooking. If they are unavailable, onions may be substituted.

Sherry

Use either an Amontillado sherry or a Fino sherry when a recipe calls for dry sherry. I use Harvey's, or a similarly high quality sherry; only a small amount is needed, so it is not very expensive to use the best.

Soy Flour

Soy flour is available in all health food stores. My recipes call for full-fat soy flour which has the least amount of carbohydrates. It is also available toasted, but I don't particularly like it. The advantage of soy flour over wheat flour is that soy flour has a high protein content and a very low carbohydrate content. Old Stone Mill and Cellu were the two brands I found best. See my Seasoned Soy Flour recipe, page 22.

Stock—Chicken or Beef

Canned chicken stock and beef stock are the best substitutes for homemade. Bouillon cubes or powder may also be used, but they are usually too salty.

Sugarless Diet Jams

Be careful when buying sugarless jams. Some brands are made with sorbitol, which is not a carbohydrate-free sweetener. It just metabolizes more slowly than sugar. I suggest either Louis Sherry or Polaner's sugarless preserves. They come in a wide variety of flavors and are very good. I've used them a number of times in my recipes.

Vinegar

Always buy good quality vinegar. For salads, imported wine vinegar is the best because it's the mildest and most delicate-tasting. It is available in some supermarkets as well as in gourmet specialty shops and can be purchased flavored with shallots, garlic, tarragon, lemon, and even champagne. Rice vinegar is used for Chinese and Japanese recipes. See Chinese and Japanese Ingredients (Specialties), page 13.

Wine

Either American or French wines may be used. I generally prefer to use French dry vermouth in place of white wine as wine keeps only for two or three days, even in the refrigerator, and then turns to vinegar. Dry vermouth keeps indefinitely in the refrigerator.

TIPS FOR DIETERS

1. If you are dying for something sweet and on the verge of breaking your diet, take a tablespoonful or two of artificially sweetened jam or put a little artificial sweetener on your tongue. It will kill the craving.

2. Read labels carefully. There are hidden carbohydrates in many foods.

3. Beware of hidden carbohydrates when eating in restaurants. A friend of mine ruined her diet for months by eating generous amounts of the bottled orange-colored French dressing served in many restaurants because she thought it had no carbohydrates, not realizing it is only the oil-and-vinegar French dressing that has no carbohydrates.

4. Always leave yourself a little hungry when you leave the table and wait for at least an hour before you eat anything else. By that time, your blood sugar may have risen enough so that you'll no longer need any more food.

5. Always eat something before you go to someone's house for dinner if you don't know what is being served. This will keep you from eating fattening food just because you're hungry or because there's nothing else to eat.

6. Always choose the lowest-carbohydrate foods and beverages. You get more mileage that way.

7. If you're angry or upset, take a long walk or go to sleep instead of heading for the refrigerator. I'm lucky in this respect—when I'm upset I can't eat or stand the smell of food.

8. Become a gourmet. Eat only food that really tastes superb.

9. If you find you simply must nibble on something, try to keep cold meat and chicken, cooked lobster, shrimp and crabmeat, cheese, or a hard-cooked egg on hand for just such emergencies. When preparing dinner, cook a little extra to save for snacks.

10. Always check with your doctor before embarking on any diet or dietary regime. Make sure to take the correct vitamin and mineral supplements that he prescribes in order to meet minimum daily requirements.

I.
YES, YOU CAN BAKE WITH SOY FLOUR

Yes, You Can Bake
With Soy Flour

This chapter is my pride and joy!

Everybody has always said that it was impossible to bake using soy flour alone. These recipes prove everybody was wrong. It can be done. The advantage of using soy flour is that it is very high in protein and very low in carbohydrates. However, if it were used interchangeably with regular flour, the finished product would be so heavy that it would leave a lump in your stomach. One of the problems in developing these recipes was to make baked goods as light as those made with regular flour. I think you will agree that I succeeded.

SEASONED SOY FLOUR

Makes ¼ cup. Use this seasoned soy flour whenever a recipe calls for seasoned flour.

30 grams (¼ cup, unsifted) full-fat soy flour
½ teaspoon salt
2 dashes garlic powder
2 dashes onion powder
2 dashes ground celery seed
¼ teaspoon freshly ground black pepper

22

Combine all ingredients, mix thoroughly, and place in an airtight container. Set aside to use as needed.

9.1 grams of carbohydrate in entire recipe; makes ¼ cup, each tablespoon containing 2.9 grams of carbohydrate.

126 calories in entire recipe; makes ¼ cup, each tablespoon containing 32 calories.

BATTER FOR FRYING

Makes ½ cup

2 extra-large eggs, at room temperature, separated
¼ teaspoon cream of tartar
15 grams (2 tablespoons) full-fat soy flour
⅛ teaspoon baking powder
⅛ teaspoon salt
⅛ teaspoon ground celery seed
⅛ teaspoon black pepper
Few dashes of onion powder
2 tablespoons grated Parmesan cheese

Beat egg whites until foamy, add cream of tartar, and continue beating until whites are stiff but not dry. Beat egg yolks, then gently fold into whites. Combine soy flour with baking powder, salt, and spices and sift into eggs. Fold in gently. Fold in the Parmesan cheese.

6.0 grams of carbohydrate in entire recipe.
303 calories in entire recipe.

NOTE: Use this as a batter for either deep or shallow frying. Try deep-frying vegetables such as zucchini, eggplant, or any other ingredients commonly used in a *Fritto misto*. If desired, ingredients can be coated with additional grated Parmesan cheese before coating with batter.

EASY-MIX MUFFINS

Makes 12 muffins. These are so easy to make that even my friends who can't cook can make them.

90 grams (about ¾ cup, unsifted) full-fat soy flour
1 tablespoon baking powder
Dash of salt
3 extra-large eggs
¼ cup heavy cream
½ cup plus 1 tablespoon cold water
¼ teaspoon nutmeg, freshly grated
1½ teaspoons butter extract
1½ teaspoons vanilla extract
Granulated artificial sweetener equal to 6 tablespoons sugar

Preheat oven to 400° F. Combine soy flour, baking powder, and salt and set aside. (I usually weigh the flour in a plastic bag, add the other ingredients and then set the bag aside.) Beat eggs thoroughly, then add the cream, water, nutmeg, extracts, and sweetener. Sift in the soy flour mixture and beat until well combined. The texture should resemble sour cream.

Either grease muffin tins or fill muffin tins with special papers designed for them and divide mixture into 12 muffins. Top with Cinnamon Sugar Topping (page 229) if desired. Bake the muffins for 17 to 20 minutes or till done. Store in the refrigerator in a plastic bag when cooled. These muffins freeze beautifully and can easily be reheated in aluminum foil.

30.7 grams of carbohydrate in entire recipe; makes 12 muffins, each muffin containing 2.6 grams of carbohydrate.
909 calories in entire recipe; makes 12 muffins, each muffin containing 76 calories.

EASY-MIX MUFFINS—A VARIATION

Follow the recipe for Easy-Mix Muffins, adding in ¼ teaspoon of cinnamon and ¼ teaspoon of almond extract with the other flavorings.

CINNAMON-PECAN PUFFINS

Makes 8 puffins. Puffins are a cross between a popover and a muffin. If you've been dreaming of hot popovers, here's a worthy substitute!

1½ ounces pecans
½ teaspoon cinnamon
Granulated artificial sweetener equal to 1 tablespoon sugar
3 extra-large eggs, at room temperature, separated
30 grams (¼ cup, unsifted) full-fat soy flour
¾ teaspoon baking powder
Dash of salt
¼ teaspoon cream of tartar
3 tablespoons sour cream
¾ teaspoon butter extract
½ teaspoon vanilla extract
20 drops bitter almond extract
3 tablespoons cold water
Granulated artificial sweetener equal to ⅛ cup sugar

Chop nuts (easily done in a blender). Combine with cinnamon and granulated artificial sweetener equal to 1 tablespoon sugar and mix thoroughly. Set aside for topping.

Preheat oven to 325° F. Separate eggs. Beat egg whites with cream of tartar until stiff but not dry. Beat egg yolks till thick and lemon-colored. To egg yolks, add sour cream, extracts, artificial sweetener equal to ⅛ cup sugar, and water and beat thoroughly. Combine soy flour, baking powder, cream of tartar, and salt and sift into the yolk mixture. Stir until combined, then gently fold in the egg whites.

Grease a muffin or cupcake tin for 8 puffins. Spoon 1 tablespoon of batter into each greased section. Sprinkle a little topping mixture over this batter, then spoon in remaining batter, dividing it evenly. Top with remaining nut mixture and bake in preheated oven for 50 to 60 minutes. Cool the puffins completely in the pan (even if takes a few hours). To store, place in refrigerator in a plastic bag with 3 tiny holes punctured on each side. (Use a paring knife or fork to make the holes.) To reheat, place in moderate oven for 8 to 10 minutes.

18.4 grams of carbohydrate in entire recipe; when making 8 puffins, each puffin contains 2.3 grams of carbohydrate.
796 calories in entire recipe; when making 8 puffins, each puffin contains 100 calories each.

NOTE: For puffins with the texture of popovers, use 3 tablespoons water; for a muffin texture, use 2 tablespoons water.

CINNAMON BREAD

Makes 4 small loaves

Pam spray (page 17)
Butter or shortening for greasing
30 grams (¼ cup, unsifted) full-fat soy flour
½ teaspoon baking powder
Dash of salt
6 extra-large eggs, at room temperature, separated
¼ teaspoon cream of tartar
2 tablespoons cold water
1 teaspoon cinnamon
Granulated artificial sweetener equal to 6 tablespoons sugar
2 teaspoons butter extract

Preheat oven to 350° F. Prepare 4 small bread pans, each measuring 6 x 3½ x 2 inches, by spraying with Pam and greasing lightly. Set aside.

Sift together soy flour, baking powder, and salt and set aside. Beat egg whites until foamy, add cream of tartar, and continue beating until stiff but not dry. Beat yolks until thick and lemon-colored. To the yolks add water, cinnamon, artificial sweetener, and butter extract, beating until thoroughly combined. Sift in soy flour mixture and beat again until smooth. Fold a little of the beaten egg whites into the yolk mixture and blend thoroughly. Then very gently fold in remaining whites, being careful not to break them down.

Divide batter among the prepared pans. Place the pans in the oven and bake 1 hour. Store loaves in the refrigerator in a plastic bag, punctured with 2 or 3 small holes on each side. To serve, slice each loaf in 8 slices. Try this bread with Nutted Whipped Cream Cheese (page 230) or with cream cheese and surgarless strawberry jam.

12.8 grams of carbohydrate in entire recipe; makes 4 loaves of bread, each loaf containing 3.2 grams of carbohydrate. Assuming 8 slices of bread per loaf, each slice contains 0.4 grams of carbohydrate.

693 calories in entire recipe; makes 4 loaves of bread, each loaf containing 173 calories. Assuming 8 slices of bread per loaf, each slice contains 22 calories.

NOTE: This recipe can easily be cut in half, but as long as you are making it, it is easier to make more and freeze loaves that will not be used immediately.

CINNAMON-NUT COFFEE CAKE SQUARES

Makes 12 squares

15 grams (⅛ cup, unsifted) soy flour
¾ teaspoon baking powder
Dash of salt
1¼ teaspoons ground cinnamon
3 extra-large eggs, at room temperature, separated
¼ teaspoon cream of tartar
4 tablespoons sour cream

Granulated artificial sweetener equal to ½ cup plus 1 tablespoon sugar
½ teaspoon vanilla extract
½ teaspoon butter extract
½ cup finely chopped pecans or walnuts
2 tablespoons melted butter

Preheat oven to 350° F. Combine soy flour, baking powder, cinnamon, and salt and set aside. Beat egg whites until frothy, add cream of tartar, and continue beating till stiff but not dry. In another bowl, beat egg yolks at high speed with an electric mixer until thick and lemon-colored (about 5 minutes). Add to the yolks the sour cream, sweetener, and extracts and beat 1 to 2 minutes more. Sift in soy flour mixture and beat till smooth. Gently fold in the egg whites and then the nuts. Pour batter into a greased 8-inch square pan and bake for 5 minutes. Drizzle melted butter over the cake and bake for another 50-55 minutes. Cool cake, then cut into squares.

18.2 grams of carbohydrate in entire recipe if made with walnuts. Makes 12 squares, each square containing 1.5 grams of carbohydrate.
16.3 grams of carbohydrate in entire recipe if made with pecans, and 1.4 grams of carbohydrate per square.
1,069 calories in entire recipe if made with walnuts. Makes 12 squares, each square containing 89 calories.
1,038 calories in entire recipe if made with pecans, and 87 calories per square.

PECAN BUTTER COFFEE CAKE

Makes 18 squares

1 recipe Butter Sponge Cake (page 36)

⅔ cup finely chopped pecans
Granulated artificial sweetener equal to ¼ cup sugar
½ teaspoon ground cinnamon

Preheat oven to 325° F. Thoroughly grease a 13 x 9 x 2-inch cake pan. Pour in approximately half of the prepared cake batter. Combine chopped pecans, artificial sweetener, and cinnamon and sprinkle half of the pecan mixture evenly over the batter. Pour in remaining batter and sprinkle with remaining nut mixture. Bake 35 to 40 minutes or until cake tests done. Cool cake in the pan, then cut into squares. Place squares in a plastic bag punctured with 2 or 3 holes and refrigerate overnight to improve texture.

21.12 grams of carbohydrate in entire recipe; if making 18 squares, each square contains 1.2 grams of carbohydrate.

1,185 calories in entire recipe; if making 18 squares, each square contains 66 calories.

NOTE: Half of this recipe is perfect for an 8-inch-square pan and makes 9 squares.

EASY-MIX PANCAKES

Makes approximately 20 pancakes

90 grams (¾ cup, unsifted) full-fat soy flour
1 tablespoon baking powder
3 extra-large eggs
¼ cup heavy cream
¾ cup plus 2 tablespoons cold water
1½ teaspoons butter extract
1½ teaspoons vanilla extract
Generous dash of nutmeg
Artificial sweetener equal to 2 tablespoons sugar
Butter for frying

Combine soy flour and baking powder and set aside. Beat eggs thoroughly, then add cream, water, extracts, nutmeg, and sweetener. Sift in the soy flour mixture and beat until well combined. Grease a griddle with a tablespoon of butter and heat until a few drops of water sizzle when splashed on it. Drop the batter onto the griddle with a soup ladle. When the pancakes are puffed and full of bubbles, turn them, and brown the other side. Finished pancakes may be kept warm in a 200° F. oven. Serve hot with butter and sugarless syrup or sugarless jam.

30.7 grams of carbohydrate in entire recipe; makes approximately 20 pancakes, each pancake containing 1.6 grams of carbohydrate.

909 calories in entire recipe plus 102 calories for every tablespoon of butter used in frying; makes approximately 20 pancakes, each pancake containing 45 calories exclusive of the butter used.

NOTE: These pancakes can be made in larger quantities or in advance and frozen, wrapped in aluminum foil. Simply rewarm them in a moderate oven.

PUFFY PANCAKES

Makes 20 pancakes

30 grams (¼ cup, unsifted) full-fat soy flour
¾ teaspoon baking powder
Dash of salt
4 extra-large eggs, at room temperature, separated
½ teaspoon cream of tartar
1 cup pot cheese
½ teaspoon vanilla extract
1 teaspoon butter extract
2 dashes cinnamon
2 dashes nutmeg
2 teaspoons water
Granulated artificial sweetener equal to 2 tablespoons sugar
Butter for frying

Mix the flour, baking powder, and salt together and set aside. Separate eggs, placing yolks in a blender and whites in a bowl. Add cream of tartar to the egg whites and beat until stiff but not dry. To the yolks, add the pot cheese and remaining ingredients and blend until smooth. Empty cheese-yolk mixture into beaten egg whites and sift the flour mixture over that. Gently fold everything together.

Heat a griddle and grease it lightly. Drop batter from the tip of a large spoon onto the griddle. Bake over a low flame until pancake rises and surface is dotted with bubbles. Turn and bake the second side until golden brown. While making second and third batches, keep the finished pancakes hot in a warm oven (about 200° F.). Serve hot with dietetic syrup or dietetic jam.

17.9 grams of carbohydrate in entire recipe; if making 20 pancakes, each pancake contains 0.9 grams of carbohydrate.
760 calories in entire recipe; if making 20 pancakes, each pancake contains 38 calories. (Calorie counts exclude butter used in frying.)

NOTE: These pancakes can be wrapped in aluminum foil and frozen, then rewarmed in a moderate oven. They lose a little of their original puffiness, but are still good, especially for days when you are in a hurry.

FRENCH TOAST

Makes 2 servings of 4 pieces each

1 loaf my Cinnamon Bread (page 26)
1 egg
3 tablespoons heavy cream
3 tablespoons cold water
¼ teaspoon vanilla extract
Generous dash of freshly ground nutmeg
2 tablespoons butter

Slice the bread into 8 slices. Beat egg thoroughly, then beat in the cream, water, vanilla, and nutmeg. Dip bread slices in the egg mixture one at a time. Melt 1 tablespoon of the butter on a Teflon grill and fry the bread until golden brown on first side. Turn the slices, add a little extra butter under each, and brown the second side. Serve hot with sugarless maple syrup or sugarless diet jam.

5.1 grams of carbohydrate in entire recipe; if serving 2, each serving contains 2.6 grams for each 4-slice serving.

636 calories in entire recipe; if serving 2, each serving contains 318 calories for each 4-slice serving.

BASIC NOODLE DOUGH

Makes 4 servings. Miss your fettuccine? It's not forbidden anymore.

2 extra-large eggs, at room temperature, separated
60 grams (½ cup, unsifted) full-fat soy flour
½ teaspoon salt
15 grams (2 tablespoons, unsifted) additional soy flour
3 quarts water
1½ teaspoons salt

Beat eggs thoroughly with a fork or wire whisk. Add soy flour and salt and mix well. Place a large sheet of waxed paper on a flat surface, or use a wooden board, if you have one. Sift a tiny amount of the extra soy flour all over the waxed paper or board. Place the dough on the waxed paper, making sure that all surfaces, top and bottom, get a light coating of the soy flour. Roll out the dough with a rolling pin until very thin. (I like the French rolling pins without any handles best.) Try to roll the dough into a rectangular shape. Work fast!

Beginning with the narrow end, gently fold over about 2 inches of dough and continue turning like a jelly roll until the roll is about 3 inches thick. Dough should be dry enough so layers do not stick together, but should not have a heavy coating of extra soy flour. With a very sharp knife, cut rolled dough in even slices—¼ inch wide for fettuccine and as desired for other pasta. Unroll strips carefully so as not to break them, and arrange on waxed paper, keeping flat. The noodles may be left to dry for 1 or 2 hours, or cooked immediately.

To cook, bring water to a rolling boil. Add salt and put in the pasta, pushing it down gently until all is submerged in the water. (A little oil added will keep the pasta from sticking.) Cook to the *al dente* stage, testing frequently to make sure the pasta does not overcook. (*Al dente* means tender but still firm to bite.) Drain pasta thoroughly in a colander and use it with your favorite pasta recipe.

23.8 grams of carbohydrate in entire recipe; if serving 4, each serving contains 6.0 grams of carbohydrate.
504 calories in entire recipe; if serving 4, each serving contains 126 calories.

HERBED ROLLS

Makes 6 rolls. Try these rolls filled with chicken salad.

3 extra-large eggs, at room temperature, separated
¼ teaspoon cream of tartar
4 tablespoons cottage cheese
¼ teaspoon ground celery seed
¼ teaspoon salt
2 dashes white pepper
¼ teaspoon dill weed
½ teaspoon poppy seeds

Preheat oven to 300° F. Beat egg whites until foamy, add cream of tartar, and continue beating until stiff but not dry. Mix together egg yolks, cottage cheese, celery seed, salt, pepper, and dill weed. Very gently fold the yolk mixture into the whites. A rubber spatula is ideal for this job.

Either grease a large cookie sheet or spray it with Pam. Spoon heaping tablespoons of the batter one on top of another until you have made 6 rolls. Sprinkle the tops with poppy seeds and bake the rolls for 1 hour. Cool slightly and serve, or store in the refrigerator in a plastic bag.

2.9 grams of carbohydrate in entire recipe; makes 6 rolls, each roll containing 0.5 grams of carbohydrate.
340 calories in entire recipe; makes 6 rolls, each roll containing 57 calories.

PARMESAN PUFFS

Makes 8 puffs. These make delicious hamburger buns!

2 extra-large eggs, at room temperature, separated
¼ teaspoon cream of tartar
1 tablespoon cottage cheese
⅛ teaspoon salt
Dash of white pepper
¼ teaspoon ground celery seed
Dash of onion powder
¼ teaspoon baking powder
1 ounce Parmesan cheese, finely grated

Preheat oven to 325° F. Beat egg whites until frothy, add cream of tartar, and continue beating until stiff but not dry. In another bowl, beat egg yolks at high speed with an electric mixer until thick and lemon-yellow. Add cottage cheese, salt, pepper, celery seed, onion powder, and baking powder and beat for another minute. Fold in Parmesan cheese, then gently fold beaten egg whites into yolk-spice mixture. Drop by heaping tablespoonfuls onto a greased cookie sheet and bake for 30 minutes or until golden brown.

2.2 grams of carbohydrate in entire recipe; makes 8 puffs, each containing 0.3 grams of carbohydrate.
313 calories in entire recipe; makes 8 puffs, each containing 39 calories.

SWEET CRÊPES

Makes 16 crêpes. These crêpes are the base for Blintzes (page 46) and Flaming Crêpes (page 47).

3 eggs
3 tablespoons heavy cream
¾ cup cold water

½ teaspoon vanilla extract
1 teaspoon butter extract
Granulated artificial sweetener equal to 3 tablespoons sugar
Pinch of salt
90 grams (¾ cup, unsifted) full-fat soy flour
2 tablespoons oil or melted butter

Combine the eggs, heavy cream, cold water, vanilla extract, butter extract, artificial sweetener, salt, and soy flour in an electric blender and blend at highest speed for 1 minute. If some flour adheres to sides of blender container, scrape it down with a narrow rubber spatula and blend for 2 to 3 seconds more. Refrigerate the crêpe batter in the covered blender container for 2 hours. When removed from the refrigerator, the batter should be just thick enough to coat a wooden spoon. A tablespoon or 2 of water may be added if batter needs thinning.

With a pastry brush, brush a 6-inch crêpe pan or Teflon-coated skillet with the butter or oil. Set over medium-high heat just until the pan begins to smoke. Quickly remove the pan from the flame and pour about 3 tablespoons of the batter right into the middle of the pan. A quarter-cup measuring cup about ¾ filled is convenient for this job. Quickly tilt the pan in all directions to make the batter run all over the bottom of the pan in a thin film. Return the pan to the flame for about 1 minute. Lift crêpe edges with a metal spatula, and if the underside is a nice golden brown, turn the crêpe. Brown the other side for about ½ minute. Slide the crêpe onto aluminum foil or a warm plate. Brush the skillet with fat again, heat just to smoking, and repeat until all batter is used. For suggestions on fillings see *Jam Fillings for Crêpes or Jelly Roll*, page 49.

28.7 grams of carbohydrate in entire recipe; makes 16 crêpes, each crêpe containing 1.8 grams of carbohydrate.

760 calories in entire recipe; makes 16 crêpes, each crêpe containing 48 calories.

Sponge Cake Cream Rolls

BUTTER SPONGE CAKE CREAM ROLL

Makes 16 slices. Remember the rich, gooey cakes from your pre-diet days? Well, try this and compare!

30 grams (¼ cup, unsifted) full-fat soy flour
½ teaspoon baking powder
Dash of salt
6 extra-large eggs, at room temperature, separated
¾ teaspoon cream of tartar
1½ teaspoons butter extract
1 teaspoon vanilla extract
5 tablespoons cold water
Granulated artificial sweetener equal to ¾ cup sugar

Preheat oven to 325° F.

Combine soy flour, baking powder, and salt and set aside. Beat egg whites until foamy, add cream of tartar, and continue beating until stiff but not dry. In another bowl, beat egg yolks at high speed with an electric mixer until thick and lemon-yellow—about 5 minutes. Add extracts, water, and sweetener to egg yolks, and mix until combined. Sift soy flour mixture into egg yolk mixture and beat until smooth. Gently fold egg yolk mixture into beaten egg whites.

Line a 15½ x 10½ x 1-inch jelly-roll pan with waxed paper and grease with melted butter, shortening, or oil. Spread mixture in the prepared pan, and bake for 35 to 40 minutes, or until cake tests done when a cake tester or toothpick is inserted.

Cool cake in the pan for about 5 minutes, then turn it out on a larger sheet of waxed paper. Carefully remove baked-on paper from cake bottom and discard. Roll cake lengthwise, being careful not to break it; use waxed paper as an aid. (Rolling the cake when warm helps to prevent breakage.) When cake is cool, unroll it, and fill with desired Cream Filling. Reroll the cake. Store overnight in the refrigerator in a plastic bag as this improves the texture. This cake combines well with Chocolate Rum Cream Filling, Strawberry Cream Filling, Banana Cream Filling, and Maple Walnut Cream Filling. (See *Cream Fillings for Sponge Cake Cream Rolls,* page 51.)

12.1 grams of carbohydrate in entire recipe without filling; makes 16 slices, each slice containing 0.8 grams of carbohydrate. Add carbohydrates for chosen Cream Filling and divide by 16 to get the count per slice.

705 calories in entire recipe without filling; makes 16 slices, each slice containing 44 calories. Add calories for chosen Cream Filling and divide by 16 to get the count per slice.

NOTE: This cake may also be cut into squares and eaten as a plain Sponge Cake without filling.

ORANGE SPONGE CAKE CREAM ROLL

Perhaps you prefer orange? Follow ingredients and preparation for Butter Sponge Cake Cream Roll, adding ½ teaspoon orange extract with other extracts. This cake combines well with Orange Chocolate Cream Filling (page 55) and with Orange Brandied Cream Filling (page 54).

Carbohydrate and calorie values are the same as for Butter Sponge Cake Cream Roll above.

LEMON SPONGE CAKE CREAM ROLL

Follow directions for ingredients and preparation for Butter Sponge Cake Cream Roll, adding ½ teaspoon lemon extract with other extracts. This cake combines well with Lemon Cream Filling (page 52).

Carbohydrate and calorie values are the same as for Butter Sponge Cake Cream Roll (page 36).

ALMOND SPONGE CAKE CREAM ROLL

Follow directions for ingredients and preparation for Butter Sponge Cake Cream Roll, adding 1 teaspoon almond extract. This cake combines well with Chocolate Almond Cream Filling (page 55).

Carbohydrate and calorie values are the same as for Butter Sponge Cake Cream Roll (page 36).

GINGERBREAD SQUARES OR SPICE CAKE CREAM ROLL

Makes 18 squares. How about hot gingerbread with whipped cream?

30 grams (¼ cup, unsifted) full-fat soy flour
½ teaspoon baking powder
Dash of salt
6 extra-large eggs, at room temperature, separated
¾ teaspoon cream of tartar
7 tablespoons cold water
1½ teaspoons nutmeg
1½ teaspoons cloves
1½ teaspoons allspice

1½ teaspoons ginger
1½ teaspoons cinnamon
Granulated artificial sweetener equal to 1¼ cups sugar
½ teaspoon butter extract
½ teaspoon orange extract

To make *Gingerbread Squares*, follow directions for the preparation of Butter Sponge Cake Cream Roll batter (page 36), adding the spices at the same time as the water and extracts. Bake the cake in a 13 x 9 x 2-inch baking pan for 35 to 40 minutes. When the cake has cooled, cut it in 18 squares. To make ½ of this recipe, halve the ingredients and bake in an 8-inch square pan. Top the Gingerbread Squares with Vanilla Cream Filling (page 53) or Orange Brandied Cream Filling (page 54).

To make a *Spice Sponge Cake Cream Roll*, follow the complete preparation instructions for Butter Sponge Cake Cream Roll and bake in a jelly-roll pan. The roll can then be filled with either Vanilla Cream Filling or Orange Brandied Cream Filling.

12.1 grams of carbohydrate in entire recipe. Each slice or piece contains 0.8 grams of carbohydrate.
705 calories in entire recipe. If cut into 18 squares, each contains 39 calories.

NOTE: If you halve the Gingerbread Squares recipe, simply halve the carbohydrate and calorie counts.

BRAZIL NUT PIE CRUST

Crust for one 9-inch pie or 6 servings. Try this and see if you don't agree that Brazil nuts make the most delicious pie crust you've ever tasted.

¼ pound shelled Brazil nuts
Granulated artificial sweetener equal to 2 tablespoons sugar

Chop the Brazil nuts till very fine or grind them in a blender. Mix the Brazil nuts with the artificial sweetener and press the mixture firmly onto the bottom and sides of a greased 9-inch pie plate. Fill with desired chiffon filling and refrigerate. I like to use a glass pie plate or Corning Ware pie plate which goes to the table prettily.

12.4 grams of carbohydrate in entire recipe; if serving 6, the crust will contain 2.1 grams per serving.

742 calories in entire recipe; if serving 6, the crust will contain 124 calories per serving.

SWEET PIE CRUST (COOKIE CRUST)

Makes 6 servings. If you want a baked pie crust, try this one.

6 tablespoons sweet butter
3 ounces Farmer's cheese
Granulated artificial sweetener equal to 2 tablespoons sugar
60 grams (½ cup) full-fat soy flour, sifted
An additional 15 grams of soy flour

Preheat oven to 350° F. Cream together butter and Farmer's cheese with an electric mixer or blender. Mix in artificial sweetener. Gradually add soy flour and combine thoroughly. Wrap dough in waxed paper or plastic wrap and chill in refrigerator for 1 to 2 hours until dough is firm enough to roll.

The easiest way to roll this dough is between sheets of waxed paper, remembering to loosen both the upper and lower papers several times to prevent sticking. Place 1 sheet of waxed paper on a firm, flat surface, sift a little of the extra 15 grams of soy flour all over paper, and place ball of dough on top. Sift a bit more of remaining soy flour on top of the dough and place a second sheet of waxed paper on top. Roll dough to fit a 9-inch pie pan and invert it over the pan. Work fast. If dough should tear a little, do not reroll. (This dough may be patched.) I like to flute the edges by placing 1 finger between 2 fingers of the opposite hand and pressing the resulting design around the entire edge. This takes just a few extra minutes and looks so much prettier.

Bake the crust in the preheated oven for 12 to 14 minutes before using. This crust may also be baked with filling in it. Follow filling recipe directions.

25.0 grams of carbohydrate in entire pie crust; if serving 6, the crust for each serving contains 4.2 grams of carbohydrate.

1,039 calories in entire pie crust; if serving 6, the crust for each serving contains 173 calories.

II.
THE SWEET THINGS IN LIFE

The Sweet Things in Life

I have deliberately put my dessert chapter at the front of my book because I have found that sweets are what dieters seem to miss most. On many diets, including most low-carbohydrate diets, you can eat interesting appetizers, delicious main courses, tasty salads and vegetables, fine Continental foods, but *no* fancy desserts. This chapter gives a multitude of tasty desserts back to you—with a minimum of carbohydrates. Enjoy them and use them to lose weight as well as to stay thin.

BRANDY NUT KISSES

Makes 24 cookies

3 egg whites, at room temperature
Pinch of salt
½ teaspoon cream of tartar
1 teaspoon Cognac
Granulated artificial sweetener equal to ¾ cup sugar
1 cup very finely chopped pecans

Preheat oven to 250° F. Beat egg whites until foamy, add salt and cream of tartar, and continue beating until stiff but not dry. Add Cognac and artificial sweetener and beat 1 minute more. Very gently fold in pecans. Drop by teaspoonfuls onto a greased cookie sheet and bake approximately 30 to 35 minutes or until dry. When cooled, store cookies in an airtight container.

15.2 grams of carbohydrate in entire recipe; makes 24 kisses, each cookie containing 0.6 grams of carbohydrate.

787 calories in entire recipe; makes 24 kisses, each cookie containing 33 calories.

JAM SANDWICH COOKIES

Makes 12 cookies

2 extra-large eggs
Granulated artificial sweetener equal to 3 tablespoons sugar
¼ teaspoon butter extract
½ teaspoon lemon extract
¼ teaspoon vanilla
1 teaspoon cold water
2 ounces diet apricot jam

Preheat oven to 325° F. Beat eggs with an electric mixer at high speed until the eggs become very thick and lemon colored. This should take at least 10 minutes. Mix in artificial sweetener, extracts, and water.

Grease muffin pans (for 24) and divide mixture among the 24 spaces. Bake 10 minutes. Remove pans from oven and cool cookies.

When cookies have cooled, spread 12 of the cookies with diet apricot jam, using about 2 ounces in all. Cover these 12 cookies with the remaining 12 cookies, forming sandwich cookies. Store in the refrigerator in a plastic bag.

2.0 grams of carbohydrate in entire recipe; makes 12 cookies, each cookie containing 0.2 grams of carbohydrate.

196 calories in entire recipe; makes 12 cookies, each cookie containing 16 calories.

BLINTZES

Makes 16 blintzes. Years ago whenever I went to the old Lindy's, blintzes were my favorite dish.

1 recipe Sweet Crêpes (page 34)
1 egg
2 ounces cream cheese, softened
6 ounces Farmer's cheese, softened
Granulated artificial sweetener equal to 3 tablespoons sugar
Dash of cinnamon
Scant ½ teaspoon vanilla extract
2 tablespoons butter

Prepare crêpe batter and refrigerate at least 2 hours in advance. Cook crêpes just before making the filling for blintzes and keep warm.

Mix together in an electric mixer until smooth the egg, cream cheese, Farmer's cheese, artificial sweetener, cinnamon, and vanilla. Put about 1 rounded teaspoonful of cheese mixture in the center of each sweet crêpe and roll it up, folding in the sides to make a little sealed package. Repeat until all cheese mixture and blintzes have been used. Melt 1 tablespoon butter in a large skillet and sauté the blintzes until golden brown. Add remaining butter, turn blintzes, and brown on other side. Serve hot with sour cream and sugarless strawberry jam.

35.6 grams of carbohydrate in entire recipe; makes 16 blintzes, each blintz containing 2.2 grams of carbohydrate. Add .05 grams of carbohydrate for each tablespoon of sour cream used and .08 grams of carbohydrate for each tablespoon of sugarless jam.

1,186 calories in entire recipe; makes 16 blintzes, each blintz containing 74 calories. Add 29 calories for each tablespoon of sour cream used and 6 calories for each tablespoon of sugarless jam.

FLAMING CRÊPES

Makes 8 servings. Crêpes make an impressive dessert for company. Just don't set the house on fire when you flame them.

1 recipe Sweet Crêpes (page 34)
2 jars any Jam Filling for Crêpes or Jelly Roll (page 49)
4 tablespoons (½ stick) melted butter
4 tablespoons kirsch, Grand Marnier, or peach or apricot brandy
Additional granulated artificial sweetener

Prepare crêpe batter and refrigerate at least 2 hours in advance. Make and fill crêpes before guests arrive. Lay each crêpe on a flat surface. Place 2 teaspoons of Jam Filling in the center, roll up, and place in a shallow baking dish. When all crêpes are filled, sprinkle with the melted butter.

Just before serving, place the dish in a preheated 350° F. oven for 5 to 10 minutes to warm the crêpes. Warm the brandy or liqueur slightly. Pour warmed spirits over crêpes and ignite with a long, fireplace match or a kitchen match. When flames die down, sprinkle on a little extra granulated artificial sweetener. Serve hot.

If made with kirsch, 38.7 grams of carbohydrate in entire recipe; if serving 8, each serving contains 4.8 grams of carbohydrate.

1,691 calories in entire recipe; if serving 8, each serving contains 211 calories.

If using Grand Marnier or peach or apricot brandy, 55.4 grams of carbohydrate in entire recipe; if serving 8, each serving contains 6.9 grams of carbohydrate.

1,705 calories in entire recipe; if serving 8, each serving contains 213 calories.

JELLY ROLL

Makes 16 slices of cake. A dietetic version of an old-fashioned Jelly Roll.

1 recipe for Butter Sponge Cake (page 36) or Almond Sponge Cake (page 38)
2 cups any Jam Filling for Crêpes or Jelly Roll (page 49)

When cake has cooled completely, spread with jam filling, using a metal spatula. Roll the cake and place on an attractive serving dish. Refrigerate until serving time, then cut it in 16 slices.

If using Jam Filling made with kirsch, 20.1 grams of carbohydrate in entire recipe (with other liqueurs, 34.5 grams); makes 16 slices of cake, each slice containing 1.3 grams of carbohydrate (with other liqueurs, 2.2 grams).

If using Jam Filling made with kirsch, 823 calories in entire recipe; makes 16 slices of cake, each slice containing 52 calories. Using the other liqueurs gives about the same calorie count.

Jam Fillings for Crêpes or Jelly Roll

APRICOT JAM FILLING

Makes 1 cup. Grand Marnier is marvelous when mixed with apricot.

1 cup (8-ounce jar) sugarless apricot jam
1 tablespoon Grand Marnier or apricot brandy
Granulated artificial sweetener equal to ½ cup sugar

Mix all ingredients together thoroughly. This filling may be made in advance and stored in the refrigerator until needed.

11.2 grams of carbohydrate in entire recipe, each teaspoonful containing 0.7 grams of carbohydrate.
60 calories in entire recipe, each teaspoonful containing 4 calories.

PEACH FILLING

Makes 1 cup

1 cup (8-ounce jar) sugarless peach jam
1 tablespoon peach brandy
Granulated artificial sweetener equal to ½ cup sugar

Follow method for Apricot Jam Filling.

Carbohydrate and calorie values are the same as for Apricot Jam Filling.

CHERRY JAM FILLING

Makes 1 cup

1 cup (8-ounce jar) sugarless cherry jam
2 teaspoons kirsch
Granulated artificial sweetener equal to ¼ cup sugar

Mix all ingredients together thoroughly. This filling may be made in advance and stored in the refrigerator until needed. I generally just return it to the jam jar.

4.0 grams of carbohydrate in entire recipe, each teaspoonful containing 0.3 grams of carbohydrate.
59 calories in entire recipe, each teaspoonful containing 4 calories.

RASPBERRY JAM FILLING

Makes 1 cup

1 cup (8-ounce jar) sugarless raspberry jam
2 teaspoons kirsch
Granulated artificial sweetener equal to 3 tablespoons sugar

Mix all ingredients together thoroughly. Store in the refrigerator until needed.

Carbohydrate and calorie values are the same as for Cherry Jam Filling.

STRAWBERRY JAM FILLING

Makes 1 cup

1 cup (8-ounce jar) sugarless strawberry jam
1 teaspoon kirsch
Granulated artificial sweetener equal to 10 tablespoons sugar

Mix all ingredients together thoroughly. Store in the refrigerator to use as needed.

4.0 grams of carbohydrate in entire recipe, each teaspoonful containing 0.3 grams of carbohydrate.
46 calories in entire recipe, each teaspoonful containing 3 calories.

Cream Fillings for Sponge Cake Cream Rolls

BANANA CREAM FILLING

Filling for 16 slices of cake

12 ounces ricotta cheese
2 teaspoons banana extract
½ teaspoon vanilla extract
1 teaspoon fresh lemon juice
Artificial sweetener equal to ¼ cup sugar

Beat ricotta cheese with electric mixer until smooth and creamy. Add banana extract, vanilla, lemon juice, and sweetener and beat until well combined. Refrigerate until cake has finished baking and cooling. This filling combines well with Butter Sponge Cake (page 36).

16.0 grams of carbohydrate in entire recipe; when used as a filling for 16 slices of cake, the filling will contain 1.0 gram per slice.
605 calories in entire recipe; when used as filling for 16 slices of cake, the filling will contain 38 calories per slice.

LEMON BUTTER CREAM FILLING

Filling for 16 slices of cake

12 ounces ricotta cheese
1 teaspoon fresh lemon juice
¼ teaspoon vanilla extract
¾ teaspoon lemon extract
¼ teaspoon butter extract
½ teaspoon freshly grated lemon peel
¼ teaspoon ground mace
Artificial sweetener equal to ¼ cup sugar

Follow directions for Banana Cream Filling.

Carbohydrate values are the same as for Banana Cream Filling.
612 calories in entire recipe; when used as filling for 16 slices of cake, the
filling will contain 38 calories per slice.

MAPLE WALNUT CREAM FILLING

Filling for 16 slices of cake

12 ounces ricotta cheese
1 teaspoon maple extract
20 drops vanilla extract
Artificial sweetener equal to 6 tablespoons sugar
2½ ounces coarsely chopped walnuts (about ½ cup plus 2 tablespoons)

Follow directions for Banana Cream Filling, folding in the chopped
walnuts at the very end.

26.9 grams of carbohydrate in entire recipe; when used as filling for 16 slices
of cake, the filling will contain 1.7 grams per slice.
1,071 calories in entire recipe; when used as filling for 16 slices of cake, the
filling will contain 67 calories per slice.

STRAWBERRY CREAM FILLING

Filling for 16 slices of cake

12 ounces ricotta cheese
1 teaspoon vanilla extract
Artificial sweetener equal to 6 tablespoons sugar
1 cup fresh strawberries, sliced

Follow directions for Banana Cream Filling, folding in the strawberries at the very end.

27.7 grams of carbohydrate in entire recipe; when used as filling for 16 slices of cake, the filling will contain 1.7 grams per slice.
661 calories in entire recipe; when used as filling for 16 slices of cake, the filling will contain 41 calories per slice.

VANILLA CREAM FILLING

Filling for 16 slices of cake

12 ounces ricotta cheese
1 scant teaspoon vanilla extract
Artificial sweetener equal to 6 tablespoons sugar

Follow directions for Banana Cream Filling.

15.6 grams of carbohydrate in entire recipe; when used as filling for 16 slices of cake, the filling will contain 1.0 gram per slice.
608 calories in entire recipe; when used as filling for 16 slices of cake, the filling will contain 38 calories per slice.

NOTE: Try topping your hot gingerbread with this instead of whipped cream.

ORANGE BRANDIED CREAM FILLING

Filling for 16 slices of cake

12 ounces ricotta cheese
1¼ teaspoons orange extract
1¼ teaspoons Cognac
¼ teaspoon butter extract
Artificial sweetener equal to 6 tablespoons sugar
3 drops red food coloring
9 drops yellow food coloring

Follow directions for Banana Cream Filling. This filling combines
well with Orange Sponge Cake (page 37).

**15.6 grams of carbohydrate in entire recipe; when used as a filling for 16
slices of cake, the filling will contain 1.0 gram per slice.**
**636 calories in entire recipe; when used as a filling for 16 slices of cake, the
filling will contain 40 calories per slice.**

CHOCOLATE RUM CREAM FILLING

Filling for 16 slices of cake

12 ounces ricotta cheese
1 square unsweetened chocolate, melted
4 teaspoons chocolate extract
10 drops mocha extract
½ teaspoon rum extract
1 tablespoon dark rum
Artificial sweetener equal to ½ cup sugar

Beat ricotta cheese with electric mixer until smooth and creamy.
Melt chocolate and beat in immediately. Add extracts, rum, and
sweetener and beat till well combined. Refrigerate until cake has
finished baking and cooling. This filling combines well with Butter
Sponge Cake (page 36).

23.3 grams of carbohydrate in entire recipe; when used as filling for 16 slices of cake, the filling will contain 1.5 grams per slice.

766 calories in entire recipe; when used as filling for 16 slices of cake, the filling will contain 48 calories per slice.

NOTE: This may also be served in dessert dishes as Chocolate Rum Ricotta Mousse.

ORANGE CHOCOLATE CREAM FILLING

Filling for 16 slices of cake

12 ounces ricotta cheese
1 square unsweetened chocolate, melted
4 teaspoons chocolate extract
½ teaspoon orange extract
1 teaspoon Cognac
Artificial sweetener equal to ½ cup sugar

Follow directions for Chocolate Rum Cream Filling.

Carbohydrate values are the same as for Chocolate Rum Cream Filling.
746 calories in entire recipe; when used as filling for 16 slices of cake, the filling will contain 47 calories.

CHOCOLATE ALMOND CREAM FILLING

Filling for 16 slices of cake

12 ounces ricotta cheese
1 square unsweetened chocolate, melted
5 teaspoons chocolate extract
½ teaspoon almond extract

½ teaspoon vanilla extract
Scant ¼ teaspoon mocha extract
Artificial sweetener equal to ½ cup sugar

Follow directions for Chocolate Rum Cream Filling. This filling combines well with Almond Sponge Cake (page 38).

23.3 grams of carbohydrate in entire recipe; when used as filling for 16 slices of cake, the filling will contain 1.5 grams per slice.
736 calories in entire recipe; when used as a filling for 16 slices of cake, the filling will contain 46 calories per slice.

STRAWBERRY SHORTCAKE

Makes 8 servings. An old favorite in a new dietetic version.

1 recipe Butter Sponge Cake (page 36) or Almond Butter Sponge Cake (page 38)
300 grams (about 10½ ounces) fresh strawberries
1 egg white from an extra-large egg, at room temperature
⅛ teaspoon cream of tartar
Granulated artificial sweetener equal to 2 tablespoons sugar
1 cup day-old heavy cream

Preheat oven to 325° F. and line the bottoms of two 9-inch layer cake pans with waxed paper. (Trace the pan outline with a sharp instrument like a pair of scissors, then cut out the waxed paper circle.) Grease the pans, paper and all.

Prepare batter for sponge cake and divide equally between the 2 pans. Bake in preheated oven 35 minutes.

When the cakes are done, cool 10 minutes, then unmold from the pan, removing the waxed paper, and cool completely. Baking may be done earlier in the day. Then, wrap the cake in aluminum foil after cooling and refrigerate until ready to serve.

Wash and hull the strawberries. Set aside the 7 largest and most beautiful for decorating the top of the cake. Slice remaining berries.

Beat the egg white until foamy, add cream of tartar and artificial sweetener equal to 1 tablespoon sugar and continue beating until stiff but not dry. Set aside.

Whip the cream with artificial sweetener equal to 1 tablespoon sugar, then gently fold together the whipped cream and beaten egg white. Spread approximately a third of this mixture on 1 layer of cake. Add the sliced strawberries, combining them with the cream. Top with the second layer of cake. Spread the remaining cream mixture first on the sides and then on the top of the cake. Decorate with the whole strawberries.

Refrigerate carefully until serving time.

45.3 grams of carbohydrate in entire recipe; if serving 8, each serving contains 5.7 grams of carbohydrate.

1,830 calories in entire recipe; if serving 8, each serving contains 229 calories.

NOTE: To whip cream easily, first chill the bowl and beaters. Make sure cream is very cold and at least one day old.

INDIVIDUAL STRAWBERRY SHORTCAKES

Makes 4 servings

4 Easy-Mix Muffins (page 24)
400 grams fresh strawberries (about 14 ounces)
4 teaspoons Cognac
20 drops orange extract (¼ teaspoon)
Granulated artificial sweetener equal to ¼ cup sugar
1 egg white
⅛ teaspoon cream of tartar
1 cup day-old heavy cream
Granulated artificial sweetener equal to 2 tablespoons sugar

Slice each muffin in half. Reserve 12 of the prettiest whole strawberries. Mash remaining strawberries and add the Cognac, orange extract, and artificial sweetener equal to ¼ cup of sugar. Mix thoroughly and set aside.

Beat the egg white till foamy, add cream of tartar and continue beating until stiff but not dry. Using same beater (don't wash it), whip the cream with artificial sweetener equal to 2 tablespoons sugar. Gently fold beaten egg white into whipped cream.

Place a muffin half in each of 4 dishes. Top with a generous scoop of the cream mixture, then top cream with some mashed strawberries, dividing the berries evenly among the 4 portions. Blend the strawberries into the cream slightly by moving a teaspoon around each. Top each with the other muffin half. Spoon remaining cream over all 4 portions. Decorate with 3 whole strawberries on top of each shortcake, and refrigerate until ready to serve.

51.0 grams of carbohydrate in entire recipe; if serving 4, each serving contains 12.9 grams of carbohydrate.

1,394 calories in entire recipe; if serving 4, each serving contains 349 calories.

NOTE: These strawberry shortcakes are a little higher in carbohydrates and calories than some of my other desserts, but if you have muffins in the house as I always do, they can be made in an emergency when you have nothing else for dessert that is non-fattening. Great for unexpected company, which is the origin of this recipe, and actually it's the fruit that provides most of the carbohydrates.

Cheesecakes

CHEESECAKE SUPREME

Makes 12 servings

6 extra-large eggs, at room temperature, separated
2 teaspoons vanilla extract
1 teaspoon fresh lemon juice

¼ teaspoon ground cinnamon
½ teaspoon fresh orange peel
½ teaspoon fresh lemon peel
Granulated artificial sweetener equal to 1¼ cups sugar
½ pound cream cheese
1½ pounds Farmer's cheese
¾ teaspoon cream of tartar

Preheat oven to 325° F.

In a blender, combine egg yolks, vanilla, lemon juice, cinnamon, orange peel, lemon peel, and artificial sweetener and blend thoroughly. Add cream cheese to blender a third at a time and blend thoroughly after each addition. Add the Farmer's cheese gradually in the same way and continue to blend until smooth.

This is a very thick mixture and should be blended at the highest speed. When half the Farmer's cheese has been added and the action slows, stop the blender and use a slim rubber spatula to push the ingredients from the container sides and to stir up from the bottom. Be sure to turn the motor off before using the rubber spatula.

Beat egg whites until foamy, add cream of tartar, and continue beating until stiff but not dry. Gently fold the cheese mixture into the beaten whites.

Grease a 2½-quart baking dish or springform pan and fill with cheesecake mixture. Bake at 325° F. 15 minutes, then raise temperature to 425° F. and continue baking another 8 minutes. Turn off the oven, leaving the cake in it.

Gradually open the oven door, a little at a time. Open a little more every 5 or 10 minutes until the oven door is completely open. The cake should sit in the oven for about 1 hour after the oven has been turned off. To improve both the taste and the texture of the cake, refrigerate overnight.

30.1 grams of carbohydrate in entire recipe; if serving 12, each serving contains 2.5 grams of carbohydrate.

2,533 calories in entire recipe. If serving 12, each serving contains 211 calories.

MARBLE CHEESECAKE

Makes 10 servings

Cheesecake Batter

6 eggs
2 tablespoons lemon juice
2 teaspoons vanilla extract
4 teaspoons peanut oil
Granulated artificial sweetener equal to 1 cup sugar
2 pounds very dry pot cheese

Marble Mixture

½ cup cheesecake batter
Granulated artificial sweetener equal to 1½ cups sugar
1 teaspoon vanilla extract
2 tablespoons chocolate extract
1 ounce (1 square) unsweetened chocolate, melted
Food coloring, if desired

Preheat oven to 350° F. Have all ingredients at room temperature. In a blender, combine eggs, lemon juice, vanilla, oil, and artificial sweetener and blend thoroughly. Add pot cheese gradually and continue to blend until very smooth. Grease a 9 x 5 x 3-inch loaf pan and pour batter into it, reserving ½ cup batter in the blender container.

To make the marble mixture, add to reserved cheesecake batter the artificial sweetener, extracts, and melted chocolate and blend until combined. Add food coloring, if desired, to deepen the chocolate color. Gently drop spoonfuls of marble mixture on cheesecake batter in the prepared pan. Cut through batter with a knife or metal spatula several times for a marbled effect. Bake 40 minutes or until cake is firm. Turn off the oven, leaving the cake in it.

Gradually open the oven door, a little at a time, every 5 or 10 minutes until door is completely open. Cake should sit in the oven for about 1 to 1½ hours from the time the oven is turned off. Chill cake overnight to develop the flavor. The cake will settle as it cools.

29 grams of carbohydrate in entire recipe; if serving 10, each serving contains 2.9 grams of carbohydrate.

1,578 calories in entire recipe; if serving 10, each serving contains 157 calories.

REFRIGERATOR ITALIAN CHEESECAKE

Makes 10 servings. My version of an Italian Cheesecake that doesn't need to be baked.

1 envelope unflavored gelatin
½ cup cold water
3 tablespoons heavy cream
1 extra-large egg, at room temperature, separated
Dash of salt
1 pound ricotta cheese
1 teaspoon vanilla extract
½ teaspoon almond extract
½ teaspoon freshly grated lemon peel
Granulated artificial sweetener equal to ½ cup plus 2 tablespoons sugar
⅛ teaspoon cream of tartar

Soften gelatin in cold water for 5 minutes in the top of a double boiler. Add cream, egg yolk, and salt and heat, stirring frequently with a wire whisk, until the mixture thickens. (Do not allow to boil.) Cool the mixture slightly and empty it into a blender. Add the ricotta, vanilla and almond extracts, lemon peel, and artificial sweetener and blend until smooth and well combined. Beat egg white till foamy, add cream of tartar, and continue beating until stiff but not dry. Fold in the ricotta mixture and the lemon peel. Place the batter in a 9 x 5 x 3-inch glass or a Corning Ware loaf pan and refrigerate until firm.

21.3 grams of carbohydrate in entire recipe; if serving 10, each serving contains 2.1 grams of carbohydrate.

1,097 calories in entire recipe; if serving 10, each serving contains 110 calories.

REFRIGERATOR BANANA CHEESECAKE

Makes 8 servings

2 envelopes unflavored gelatin
1¼ cups water
2 extra-large eggs, at room temperature, separated
¼ teaspoon salt
2 tablespoons lemon juice
Granulated artificial sweetener equal to 2 cups sugar
4 teaspoons banana extract
½ teaspoon vanilla extract
½ teaspoon almond extract
24 ounces (1½ pounds) cottage cheese
¼ teaspoon cream of tartar

Put gelatin into blender with ½ cup cold water and stir to dissolve gelatin. Combine remaining water, egg yolks, salt, and lemon juice in the top of a double boiler and heat, stirring frequently, until slightly thickened. Remove from stove and add to blender. Add artificial sweetener and extracts and stir again. Raise blender speed higher, and add cottage cheese, about 8 ounces at a time and blend until smooth, but not watery.

Beat egg whites until foamy, add cream of tartar, and continue beating until stiff but not dry. Gently fold beaten egg whites into cheese mixture. Butter a cake pan or a mold, then rinse with ice cold water. Shake out any excess water, but do not dry it. Empty cheesecake mixture into prepared pan and refrigerate until firm. To serve, unmold onto a serving dish and garnish with fresh strawberries.

20.2 grams of carbohydrate in entire recipe; if serving 8, each serving contains 2.5 grams of carbohydrate.
949 calories in entire recipe; if serving 8, each serving contains 119 calories.

REFRIGERATOR LEMON CHEESECAKE

Makes 8 servings

2 envelopes unflavored gelatin
1¼ cups cold water
2 extra-large eggs, at room temperature, separated
¼ teaspoon salt
2 tablespoons lemon juice
Artificial sweetener equal to 2½ cups sugar
1 teaspoon vanilla extract
½ teaspoon lemon extract
2 teaspoons freshly grated lemon peel
1 teaspoon freshly grated orange peel
24 ounces (1½ pounds) cottage cheese
¼ teaspoon cream of tartar

Follow directions for Refrigerator Banana Cheesecake, adding lemon peel and orange peel to the blender along with the extracts.

20.2 grams of carbohydrate in entire recipe; if serving 8, each serving contains 2.5 grams of carbohydrate.
949 calories in entire recipe; if serving 8, each serving contains 119 calories.

RHUBARB SAUCE OR STEWED RHUBARB

Makes 5 servings

3 pounds rhubarb
½ cup water
1 tablespoon plus ½ teaspoon fresh lemon juice
¼–½ teaspoon cinnamon
1½ teaspoons vanilla extract
Artificial sweetener equal to 1 cup plus 2 tablespoons sugar

Wash rhubarb, trim, and cut in 1-inch pieces. Pull off any skin that is too tough to cut, stripping it down the length of the stalk. Place in a saucepan over very low heat. Add the water, lemon juice, and cinnamon, cover, and cook gently until tender and juicy, about 20 to 25 minutes. Remove from heat and add vanilla and artificial sweetener. Cool slightly, then place in a blender and purée 1 or 2 minutes until it becomes smooth sauce. This can be eaten either warm or cold.

24.2 grams of carbohydrate in entire recipe; if serving 5, each serving contains 4.8 grams of carbohydrate.
115 calories in entire recipe; if serving 5, each serving contains 23 calories.

NOTE: If you prefer a more roughly-textured rhubarb sauce, omit the blending.

Dessert Omelets

Before making any of these omelets, see General Directions for Omelet Making, page 155.

SWEET PUFFY OMELET

Makes 1 or 2 servings. A delicate, elegant sweet omelet.

2 extra-large eggs, at room temperature, separated
Artificial sweetener equal to 1 teaspoon sugar
¼ teaspoon vanilla extract
2 tablespoons unsalted butter
Additional granulated artificial sweetener for sprinkling on top

Beat egg whites until stiff but not dry. Add sweetener and vanilla to egg yolks and beat until thickened. Very gently, with a rubber spatula, fold yolk mixture into beaten egg whites.

Melt butter over high heat in a 10-inch treated or Teflon-lined omelet pan. When butter begins to brown slightly, pour in egg mixture and smooth it out evenly to the pan edges. Reduce heat to moderately low. When the bottom of the omelet is golden brown (lift edges with spatula to see) and the top somewhat puffy, turn omelet out onto a warmed platter. To do this, slide omelet halfway onto platter, then fold remaining half over it. Sprinkle top generously with powdered sweetener and serve immediately.

1.0 grams of carbohydrate in entire recipe; if serving 2, each portion contains 0.5 grams of carbohydrate.
390 calories in entire recipe; if serving 2, each portion contains 195 calories.

NOTE: Before folding the omelet over, you may spread the top with a sugarless jam, or you can serve some sugarless jam along with the omelet.

SWEET PUFFY ALMOND OMELET

Makes 1 or 2 servings

2 extra-large eggs, at room temperature, separated
15 drops almond extract
Granulated artificial sweetener equal to 2 teaspoons sugar
2 tablespoons sweet butter
Additional granulated artificial sweetener to sprinkle on top
1 tablespoon slivered, toasted almonds

Follow directions for Sweet Puffy Omelet (page 65), adding the almond extract to the egg yolks. Sprinkle the finished omelet with the toasted almonds before sprinkling with the sweetener.

2.5 grams of carbohydrate in entire recipe; if serving 2, each serving contains 1.3 grams of carbohydrate.
438 calories in entire recipe; if serving 2, each serving contains 219 calories.

SWEET PUFFY LEMON OMELET

Makes 1 or 2 servings

2 extra-large eggs, at room temperature, separated
15 drops lemon extract
1 teaspoon fresh lemon juice

1 teaspoon freshly grated lemon peel
Granulated artificial sweetener equal to 2 teaspoons sugar
2 tablespoons sweet butter
Additional granulated artificial sweetener to sprinkle on top

Follow directions for Sweet Puffy Omelet (page 65), adding the lemon peel, lemon juice, extract and artificial sweetener to the egg yolks. Turn out omelet and sprinkle with granulated sweetener.

1.4 grams of carbohydrate in entire recipe; if serving 2, each portion contains 0.7 grams of carbohydrate.
389 calories in entire recipe; if serving 2, each portion contains 195 calories.

STRAWBERRY DESSERT OMELET

Makes 2 servings. Looking for something unusual to serve for Saturday or Sunday brunch?

1 cup coarsely chopped fresh strawberries
Granulated artificial sweetener equal to 3 tablespoons sugar
1 tablespoon artificially sweetened diet apricot jam, melted
2 extra-large eggs, at room temperature, separated
¼ teaspoon cream of tartar
⅛ teaspoon vanilla extract
Dash of salt
1 tablespoon butter for frying
2 whole strawberries for garnish

Combine chopped strawberries and 1 tablespoon artificial sweetener and set aside. Combine melted jam and 1 tablespoon artificial sweetener and set aside.

Beat egg whites with cream of tartar until stiff but not dry. Without washing beater, beat egg yolks till they are thick and lemon colored. Add vanilla, remaining 1 tablespoon artificial sweetener, and salt and beat thoroughly. Gently fold beaten egg whites into beaten yolks.

Melt the butter in a hot omelet pan, turning to coat bottom and sides of pan. Pour in eggs. Lower heat and cook omelet until golden brown on the bottom and well puffed up. Spread the chopped strawberries over half the omelet, fold over remaining half, and turn out onto a warm platter. Top with the melted jam and garnish with whole strawberries.

14.0 grams of carbohydrate in entire recipe; if serving 2, each serving contains 7.0 grams of carbohydrate.
348 calories in entire recipe; if serving 2, each serving contains 174 calories.

NOTE: Strawberry jam or orange marmalade are nice with this too. Use same amount of sweetener as when using the apricot jam.

Dessert Soufflés

CHOCOLATE CHERRY SOUFFLÉ

Makes 2 servings

2 extra-large eggs, at room temperature, separated
¼ teaspoon cream of tartar
Granulated artificial sweetener equal to 2 tablespoons sugar
2 teaspoons unsweetened Dutch cocoa
2 teaspoons artificially sweetened cherry preserves
Artificial sweetener equal to 1 teaspoon sugar

Preheat oven to 375° F. Grease either a 7-inch frying pan, a 1½-cup au gratin dish, or a 1½-cup soufflé dish.

Beat egg whites until foamy, add cream of tartar, and continue beating until stiff but not dry. Beat egg yolks lightly with artificial sweetener equal to 2 tablespoons of sugar, and cocoa. Mix cherry preserves with artificial sweetener equal to 1 teaspoon sugar and spoon preserves into bottom of dish. Top with chocolate egg mixture.

Bake in preheated oven 12 to 14 minutes, or until the soufflé is well puffed. Serve immediately as this soufflé falls quickly.

4.5 grams of carbohydrate in entire recipe; if serving 2, each serving contains 2.3 grams of carbohydrate.
214 calories in entire recipe; if serving 2, each serving contains 107 calories.

LOVELY LEMON SOUFFLÉ

Makes 4 servings

4 extra-large eggs, at room temperature, separated
1 extra egg white, at room temperature
½ teaspoon cream of tartar
Granulated artificial sweetener equal to ½ cup sugar
3 tablespoons fresh lemon juice
1 tablespoon freshly grated lemon peel

Preheat oven to 400° F. Beat all 5 egg whites until foamy, add cream of tartar, and continue beating until stiff but not dry. Without washing beater, beat egg yolks until thick and lemon colored. Gradually add artificial sweetener while beating the yolks, then beat in lemon juice and lemon peel. Blend a fourth of the egg whites into the egg yolk mixture, then very gently fold in remaining whites.

Pour mixture into a buttered 1-quart soufflé dish on which you have put a waxed-paper collar. Bake for 15 to 20 minutes, depending on the degree of firmness you desire. The soufflé should be puffy and high, firm on the outside, and slightly runny inside. The longer baking time will yield a firmer soufflé.

5.6 grams of carbohydrate in entire recipe; if serving 4, each serving contains 1.4 grams of carbohydrate.
403 calories in entire recipe; if serving 4, each serving contains 101 calories.

FROZEN PUMPKIN SOUFFLÉ

Makes 6 servings. Why not try this pumpkin soufflé instead of pumpkin pie?

1 envelope unflavored gelatin
¼ cup dark rum
4 extra-large eggs, at room temperature
Granulated artificial sweetener equal to ⅔ cup sugar
1 cup pumpkin, home-cooked or canned
½ teaspoon ginger
¼ teaspoon mace
¼ teaspoon cloves
1 extra egg white, at room temperature
⅛ teaspoon cream of tartar
½ cup very cold one-day-old heavy cream

Prepare a 6-inch waxed paper or aluminum foil collar on a 1-quart soufflé dish and set aside.

In a saucepan, soften 1 envelope gelatin in ¼-cup dark rum for 5 minutes. Heat gelatin over simmering water or over gentle heat until dissolved and set aside. Beat the 4 eggs thoroughly, add artificial sweetener, and continue beating until mixture is very thick. Mix together the pumpkin, cinnamon, ginger, mace, and cloves, then add the gelatin-rum mixture to the flavored pumpkin. Mix together thoroughly.

Beat the egg white until foamy, add the cream of tartar, and continue beating until stiff but not dry. Very gently fold beaten egg white into pumpkin mixture. Whip ½ cup heavy cream, and fold gently into pumpkin mixture.

Turn soufflé into prepared dish and chill until firmly set. Remove the paper collar carefully before serving. Frozen pumpkin soufflé may be served with whipped cream that has been slightly sweetened with artificial sweetener.

24.7 grams of carbohydrate in entire recipe; if serving 6, each serving contains 4.1 grams of carbohydrate.
1,059 calories in entire recipe; if serving 6, each serving contains 177 calories.

Pudding & Pie Fillings

CHOCOLATE ALMOND PIE FILLING OR PUDDING

Filling for one 9-inch pie or 6 servings

1 envelope unflavored gelatin
½ cup heavy cream
1½ cups cold water
1 square unsweetened chocolate, melted
3 extra-large eggs, at room temperature, separated
1 teaspoon vanilla extract
½ teaspoon almond extract
Artificial sweetener equal to 1 cup sugar
¼ teaspoon cream of tartar

Soften gelatin in the cream. Boil water and add, stirring to dissolve gelatin. Mix in melted chocolate. Beat in egg yolks, 1 at a time, beating thoroughly after each addition. Place mixture in top of a double boiler or over gentle heat and cook, stirring constantly until thickened. Remove from heat and blend in extracts and artificial sweetener.

Beat egg whites until frothy, add cream of tartar, and continue beating until stiff but not dry. Gently fold beaten egg whites into chocolate mixture and turn into a pie shell or into decorative dessert dishes. Refrigerate until serving time.

12.7 grams of carbohydrate in entire recipe; if serving 6, the filling will contain 2.1 grams per serving.
877 calories in entire recipe; if serving 6, the filling will contain 146 calories per serving.

LEMON CHIFFON PIE FILLING OR PUDDING

Filling for one 9-inch pie or 6 servings. The combination of lemon chiffon with Brazil nuts is unbelievable.

1 envelope unflavored gelatin
¼ cup cold water
½ cup fresh lemon juice
Dash of salt
1–2 teaspoons freshly grated lemon peel, as desired
4 extra-large eggs, at room temperature, separated
Granulated artificial sweetener equal to 1½ cups sugar
½ teaspoon cream of tartar
Whipped cream, if desired

Soften gelatin in cold water. In the top of a double-boiler or in a heavy pot placed over gentle heat, combine lemon juice, salt, and lemon rind. Beat in the egg yolks, 1 at a time, then cook, stirring constantly, until mixture thickens and coats a spoon (it must not boil). Stir in softened gelatin. Remove from heat and add artificial sweetener.

Beat egg whites until foamy, add cream of tartar, and continue beating until stiff but not dry. Fold egg whites gently into the lemon custard. Turn into pie shell or pretty dessert dishes and chill. Top with a little whipped cream, if desired. Refrigerate until serving time.

11.9 grams of carbohydrate in entire recipe; if serving 6, the filling will contain 2.0 grams per serving.
435 calories in entire recipe; if serving 6, the filling will contain 74 calories per serving.

LIME CHIFFON PIE FILLING OR PUDDING

Filling for one 9-inch pie or 6 servings

Follow recipe for Lemon Chiffon Pie Filling, substituting ½ *cup fresh lime juice* for the fresh lemon juice, and substituting 2 *teaspoons freshly grated lime peel* for the grated lemon peel.

13 grams of carbohydrate in entire recipe; if serving 6, the filling will contain 2.2 grams per serving.
436 calories in entire recipe; if serving 6, the filling will contain 73 calories per serving.

NOTE: Both Lemon Chiffon and Lime Chiffon Pie Fillings make a nice frozen soufflé also. Prepare the soufflé dish with a waxed-paper collar. Then before bringing the soufflé to the table, remove the collar.

LEMON CAKE-PUDDING

Makes 6 servings

5 extra-large eggs
Granulated artificial sweetener equal to 1 cup sugar
3 tablespoons fresh lemon juice
Grated peel from 1 fresh lemon

Preheat oven to 325° F. Beat the eggs at high speed with an electric mixer until very thick and lemon colored. Add the sweetener and continue beating a few more minutes. Stir in, at lowest speed of the mixer, the lemon juice and lemon peel. Pour mixture into a 2-quart oven-proof soufflé dish. Set this dish into a larger pan containing 1 to

1½ inches of hot water. Bake the cake-pudding 30 minutes. Refrigerate until serving time.

6.1 grams of carbohydrate in entire recipe; if serving 6, each serving contains 1.0 gram each.
482 calories in entire recipe; if serving 6, each serving contains 80 calories.

LEMON PUDDING

Makes 5 servings. This dessert can be used for even the strictest versions of the low-carbohydrate diet. You don't have to feel deprived at all now.

1 envelope unflavored gelatin
¼ cup cold water
1½ cups boiling water
2 extra-large eggs, at room temperature, separated
Dash of salt
Granulated artificial sweetener equal to ¼ cup sugar
¼ cup lemon juice
1 teaspoon vanilla extract
Grated peel of 1 lemon
¼ teaspoon mace
¼ teaspoon cream of tartar

Soften gelatin in cold water. Add boiling water and stir until gelatin is dissolved. Pour gelatin mixture into top of a double boiler or into a heavy saucepan over gentle heat. Beat in the egg yolks, then add salt, and heat until mixture thickens. Remove from heat and add artificial sweetener, lemon juice, vanilla, lemon peel, and mace. Chill in refrigerator until mixture becomes syrupy.

Beat egg whites until frothy, add cream of tartar, and continue beating until stiff but not dry. Gently fold egg whites into lemon mixture. Rinse out a 3½–4-cup mold with icy cold water and fill with lemon pudding. Refrigerate until firm. Unmold to serve, and garnish with fresh strawberries.

5.8 grams of carbohydrate in entire recipe; if serving 5, each serving contains 1.2 grams of carbohydrate.
240 calories in entire recipe; if serving 5, each serving contains 48 calories.

RASPBERRY SPONGE PUDDING

Makes 6 servings. This delightful, fresh-tasting pudding has hardly any carbohydrates or calories.

1 envelope unflavored gelatin
½ cup cold water
1 cup fresh raspberries
1 cup boiling water
1½ teaspoons fresh lemon juice
Artificial sweetener equal to ½ cup sugar
2 egg whites, at room temperature
¼ teaspoon cream of tartar

Soften gelatin in cold water for 5 minutes. Meanwhile, crush and strain fresh raspberries. Add boiling water to gelatin and stir until gelatin is completely dissolved. Add the crushed berries, lemon juice, and artificial sweetener and mix thoroughly. Chill mixture until it thickens and becomes syrupy, then beat at high speed with an electric mixer until foamy.

Beat the egg whites until foamy, add the cream of tartar, and continue beating until stiff but not dry. Very gently fold the raspberry mixture into the egg whites, being careful not to break down the whites. Turn the sponge pudding into a pretty serving dish and chill thoroughly.

20.1 grams of carbohydrate in entire recipe; if serving 6, each serving contains 3.4 grams of carbohydrate.
142 calories in entire recipe; if serving 6, each serving contains 24 calories.

CHOCOLATE MOUSSE

Makes 8 servings. I've been told that my chocolate mousse with sugar is better than Maxim's of Paris! This sugarless version is just as good.

2 squares unsweetened chocolate
1 teaspoon unflavored gelatin
6 tablespoons cold water
4 extra-large eggs, at room temperature, separated
4 tablespoons chocolate extract
½ teaspoon mocha extract
Granulated artificial sweetener equal to 1¼ cups sugar
2 tablespoons dark rum
½ teaspoon cream of tartar

Melt chocolate over gentle heat or in a double boiler. Soften gelatin in cold water for 5 minutes. Add gelatin and water to melted chocolate. Separate the eggs, reserving the whites, and adding the yolks to the chocolate mixture. Heat the gelatin chocolate mixture gently (avoid boiling). Remove from heat and add chocolate and mocha extracts, artificial sweetener, and rum. Mix thoroughly and chill till slightly thickened but not set.

Beat egg whites until foamy, add cream of tartar, and continue beating until stiff but not dry. Gently fold beaten egg whites into chilled chocolate mixture. Place in a decorative serving dish and refrigerate until thoroughly chilled.

17.4 grams of carbohydrate in entire recipe; if serving 8, each serving contains 2.2 grams of carbohydrate.
719 calories in entire recipe; if serving 8, each serving contains 90 calories.

LEMON MOUSSE

Makes 2 servings

2 egg yolks, at room temperature
2½ tablespoons fresh lemon juice
1 teaspoon fresh lemon peel
Granulated artificial sweetener equal to ¼ cup sugar
1 egg white, at room temperature
⅛ teaspoon cream of tartar
¼ cup heavy cream, well chilled
½ cup fresh strawberries, sliced
2 large, fresh, beautiful strawberries for garnish
Sprigs of fresh mint (optional)

Beat egg yolks at highest speed with an electric mixer until they are thick and lemon colored. Beat in lemon juice and lemon peel. Do not use bottled lemon juice for this as the results will not be the same. Heat mixture over gentle heat or in the top of a double boiler until thick, stirring constantly. Let mixture cool and add artificial sweetener.

Beat egg whites till foamy, add cream of tartar, and continue beating until stiff but not dry. Gently fold egg white into lemon mixture. Whip the cream and gently fold in. Fold in sliced strawberries.

Spoon mixture into 2 parfait or wine glasses. Top each with a fresh, whole strawberry and a sprig of fresh mint. Refrigerate the mousse and chill thoroughly.

10.1 grams of carbohydrate in entire recipe; if serving 2, each serving contains 5.0 grams of carbohydrate.

423 calories in entire recipe; if serving 2, each serving contains 212 calories.

Ice Creams

VANILLA ICE CREAM

Makes 8 servings

½ cup heavy cream
4 teaspoons unflavored gelatin
Dash of salt
2 extra-large eggs, at room temperature, separated
12 ounces ricotta cheese
1 tablespoon vanilla extract
Granulated artificial sweetener equal to ¾ cup sugar
¼ teaspoon cream of tartar

Combine cream, gelatin, salt, and egg yolks in the top of a double boiler or in a saucepan over gentle heat. Heat, stirring constantly, until gelatin dissolves and mixture is smooth, then place in a blender and add ricotta cheese, vanilla, and sweetener. Blend at high speed until smooth but not watery.

Beat egg whites until frothy, add cream of tartar, and beat until stiff but not dry. Empty ricotta mixture into egg whites and gently fold together. Rinse 2 ice trays with icy cold water, shake off excess and fill with ice cream. Cover trays with aluminum foil and place in refrigerator freezing compartment at coldest setting for 1 hour. Lower temperature setting to normal after 1 hour and freeze until firm.

20.2 grams of carbohydrate in entire recipe; makes 2 trays of ice cream, each tray containing 10.1 grams of carbohydrate. If serving 8 (4 servings per tray), each serving contains 2.5 grams of carbohydrate.

1,227 calories in entire recipe; makes 2 trays of ice cream, each tray containing 639 calories. If serving 8 (4 servings per tray), each serving contains 157 calories.

CHOCOLATE ICE CREAM

Makes 8 servings

½ cup heavy cream
4 teaspoons unflavored gelatin
Dash of salt
2 extra-large eggs, at room temperature, separated
1 square unsweetened chocolate, melted
2 tablespoons plus 2 teaspoons chocolate extract
½ teaspoon vanilla extract
¼ teaspoon mocha extract
Granulated artificial sweetener equal to 1½ cups sugar
12 ounces ricotta cheese
Food coloring to make a chocolate-brown shade
¼ teaspoon cream of tartar

Follow method for Vanilla Ice Cream, adding chocolate, and extracts to gelatin mixture after it has been removed from the heat, but before combining in the blender with the ricotta cheese. After the ricotta has been blended into the mixture, add food coloring as desired to deepen the chocolate color.

27.8 grams of carbohydrate in entire recipe; makes 2 trays of ice cream, each tray containing 13.9 grams of carbohydrate. If serving 8 (4 servings per tray), each serving contains 3.5 grams.

1,393 calories in entire recipe; makes 2 trays of ice cream, each tray containing 697 calories. If serving 8 (4 servings per tray), each serving contains 174 calories.

COFFEE ICE CREAM

Makes 8 servings

½ cup heavy cream
4 teaspoons unflavored gelatin
Dash of salt
2 extra-large eggs, at room temperature, separated
12 ounces ricotta cheese
1 tablespoon instant coffee
Granulated artificial sweetener equal to 1¼ cups sugar
¼ teaspoon cream of tartar

Follow instructions for Vanilla Ice Cream, adding the instant coffee to the blender before adding the ricotta.

20.1 grams of carbohydrate in entire recipe; makes 2 trays of ice cream, each tray containing 10.1 grams of carbohydrate. If serving 8 (4 servings per tray), each serving contains 2.5 grams of carbohydrate.
1,253 calories in entire recipe; makes 2 trays of ice cream, each tray containing 677 calories. If serving 8 (4 servings per tray), each serving contains 169 calories.

MAPLE WALNUT ICE CREAM

Makes 8 servings

½ cup heavy cream
4 teaspoons unflavored gelatin
Dash of salt
2 extra-large eggs, at room temperature, separated
12 ounces ricotta cheese
1½ teaspoons maple extract
20 drops vanilla extract

Granulated artificial sweetener equal to ¾ cup sugar
¼ teaspoon cream of tartar
2 ounces finely chopped walnuts

Follow method for Vanilla Ice Cream, adding maple extract at the same time as vanilla. Fold in walnuts after you fold in egg white.

28.5 grams of carbohydrate in entire recipe; makes 2 trays of ice cream, each tray containing 14.3 grams of carbohydrate. If serving 8 (4 servings per tray), each serving contains 3.6 grams.

1,621 calories in entire recipe; makes 2 trays of ice cream, each tray containing 811 calories. If serving 8 (4 servings per tray), each serving contains 203 calories.

STRAWBERRY ICE CREAM

Makes 8 servings

½ cup heavy cream
4 teaspoons unflavored gelatin
Dash of salt
2 extra-large eggs, at room temperature, separated
1½ teaspoons vanilla extract
Granulated artificial sweetener equal to 1 cup sugar
12 ounces ricotta cheese
1 cup sliced fresh strawberries
12 drops red food coloring
¼ teaspoon cream of tartar

Follow method for Vanilla Ice Cream, adding strawberries and food coloring to the blender *after* adding the ricotta.

32.2 grams of carbohydrate in entire recipe; makes 2 trays of ice cream, each tray containing 16.1 grams of carbohydrate. If serving 8 (4 servings per tray), each serving contains 4.0 grams.

1,318 calories in entire recipe; makes 2 trays of ice cream, each tray containing 659 calories. If serving 8 (4 servings per tray), each serving contains 165 calories.

ZABAGLIONE

Makes 4 servings

6 egg yolks
¼ cup dry sherry
¼ cup Chablis or similar dry white wine
Granulated artificial sweetener equal to 5–6 tablespoons sugar

Combine egg yolks and wines in the top of a double boiler. Keep heat very low so water in the lower boiler simmers, but does not boil. Beat the mixture very gently with a wire whisk, and keep moving the cooked zabaglione to the center of the pan and moving the uncooked part to the sides. Mixture will rise and thicken, but must not boil. Once the zabaglione has risen, remove from heat, and beat in artificial sweetener very briefly.

Serve immediately, while warm, in long-stemmed glasses. For a nice variation, spoon a little sweetened icy cold whipped cream into the bottom of the glasses and top this with the hot zabaglione.

2.7 grams of carbohydrate in entire recipe; if serving 4, each serving contains 0.7 grams of carbohydrate.
542 calories in entire recipe; if serving 4, each serving contains 137 calories.

FRIO, FRIO

Can be made to serve any number of people. A quick, easy cooler.

Crushed ice
No-Cal Syrup—any flavor, or any other sugarless, no-carbohydrate syrup

Crush ice. This is easy to do in a blender if you first put in 1 full cup of water. Drain off excess water. Place crushed ice in a dessert dish.

Pour any flavor syrup over the crushed ice and eat immediately with a spoon.

Carbohydrate and calorie values are so low they need not be counted at all.

NOTE: This is an inexpensive cooler. Frio is Spanish for cold. In Spanish-speaking countries and Spanish-speaking neighborhoods in New York, it is made with a paper cup full of crushed ice and sold on the streets. Another name for these is Snow-Cones or Snowballs. Fruit-flavored syrups are customarily used.

ICE POPS

Makes 1 ice cube tray of ice pops. Do you miss the ice pops you used to buy from the Good Humor man?

2 cups fruit-flavored dietetic soda
1 envelope artificially sweetened dietetic gelatin, same flavor as soda
Artificial sweetener equal to 1 cup sugar

Bring 1 cup of soda to a boil. Remove from heat and stir in gelatin. Mix until gelatin is dissolved, then add remaining soda and artificial sweetener. Chill gelatin mixture until cooled but not set. Pour into an ice cube tray—the plastic kind with individual cubes is good. Place a plastic toothpick in each section and freeze until solid.

To unmold, twist tray and ice pops should pop out. If necessary, place tray, bottom side up, under warm water for a moment. Store ice pops in a plastic bag in the freezer.

Negligible grams of carbohydrate in the entire recipe.
40 calories per tray; if ice cube tray contains 14 spaces, each ice pop will contain 3 calories.

Some Sweet Diet Drinks

VANILLA MILK SHAKE

Makes 3½ cups. Do you still think that a cheeseburger and a milk shake make the best lunch of all?

¼ cup heavy cream
¼ cup cold water
12 ounces ricotta cheese
4 ice cubes
2 generous teaspoons vanilla extract
Artificial sweetener equal to ¼ cup sugar

Place all ingredients in a blender and blend at highest speed until thoroughly mixed and frothy. Store in the refrigerator and use as desired from the blender container, blending it again 1 or 2 seconds before each use. This is an excellent way to get nourishment at times when you may not feel like eating, or at times when you are in a hurry, since it can be made the night before.

17.4 grams of carbohydrate in entire recipe; makes 3½ cups of milk shake when blended, each cup containing 5.0 grams of carbohydrate.
826 calories in entire recipe; makes 3½ cups of milk shake when blended, each cup containing 236 calories.

VANILLA MILK SHAKE—A MORE DIETETIC VARIATION

Makes 3 cups. This milk shake has even fewer carbohydrates and fewer calories. I personally prefer it.

¼ cup heavy cream
½ cup cold water
6 ounces ricotta cheese
4 ice cubes
1 teaspoon vanilla extract
Artificial sweetener equal to ¼ cup sugar

Follow directions for Vanilla Milk Shake.

9.6 grams of carbohydrate in entire recipe; makes 3 cups of milk shake when blended, each cup containing 3.2 grams of carbohydrate.
526 calories in entire recipe; makes 3 cups of milk shake when blended, each cup containing 175 calories.

COFFEE MILK SHAKE

Makes 3 cups. A milk shake for the coffee lovers. Makes a quick, delicious breakfast.

¼ cup heavy cream
½ cup cold water
6 ounces ricotta cheese
4 ice cubes
1½ teaspoons instant coffee
Granulated artificial sweetener equal to 6 tablespoons sugar

Follow the directions for Vanilla Milk Shake, adding instant coffee to the blender with the other ingredients.

10.1 grams of carbohydrate in entire recipe; makes 3 cups of milk shake when blended, each cup containing 3.4 grams of carbohydrate.
524 calories in entire recipe; makes 3 cups of milk shake when blended, each cup containing 175 calories.

BANANA MILK SHAKE

Makes 3 cups

¼ cup heavy cream
½ cup cold water
6 ounces ricotta cheese
4 ice cubes
1 tablespoon banana extract
¼ teaspoon vanilla extract
¼ teaspoon lemon juice
Granulated artificial sweetener equal to 6 tablespoons sugar

Follow directions for Vanilla Milk Shake, adding the banana extract to the blender with the other ingredients.

9.5 grams of carbohydrate in entire recipe; makes 3 cups when blended, each cup containing 3.2 grams of carbohydrate.
522 calories in entire recipe; makes 3 cups when blended, each cup containing 174 calories.

CHOCOLATE EGG CREAM

Makes 1 serving

Ice cubes
1 cup sugarless chocolate soda, chilled
2 teaspoons heavy cream

Fill a tall glass with ice cubes. Pour the soda over the ice cubes. Mix in the cream and serve immediately with a straw.

0.3 grams of carbohydrate in entire recipe; makes 1 serving.
40 calories in entire recipe; makes 1 serving.

NATALIE'S ICED COFFEE

Makes 4 servings. My friend Natalie has this coffee for breakfast every morning.

Ice cubes
3 cups strong coffee, regular or decaffeinated
4 teaspoons heavy cream
2 teaspoons vanilla extract
Artificial sweetener to taste

Fill 4 tall glasses with ice cubes. Mix together the coffee, cream, and vanilla and fill the 4 glasses. Serve artificial sweetener alongside the iced coffee and let each person sweeten the coffee to taste.

1.7 grams of carbohydrate in entire recipe; if serving 4, each serving contains 0.4 grams of carbohydrate.
95 calories in entire recipe; if serving 4, each serving contains 24 calories.

III.
TO BEGIN A MEAL: HORS D'OEUVRE, APPETIZERS, & SOUPS

To Begin a Meal:
Hors d'Oeuvre, Appetizers, &
Soups

The appetizers included here can be used either to begin a meal or as hors d'oeuvre for parties. I have also included several of my favorite soup recipes, and if you have never tasted cold soup, you are in for a treat. Watch for other recipes elsewhere in this book such as scampi, grilled tomatoes with cheese, and various stuffed vegetables, which can also be used as a first course.

LIVER PÂTÉ

Makes 5 servings

1 pound chicken livers
¼ pound (1 stick) sweet butter
1 large onion, finely chopped
2 tablespoons dry sherry
1 tablespoon Calvados, applejack, or Cognac
1 tablespoon heavy cream

1 teaspoon salt (or to taste)
¼ teaspoon freshly ground black pepper
½ teaspoon Madras curry powder (page 15)

Wash the livers under cold water, dry with paper towels, cut in halves, and set aside.

Melt 3 tablespoons of the butter in a large, heavy skillet, add the onions, and sauté over medium heat 10 to 12 minutes, or until very soft and slightly golden. Transfer onions and pan juices to a blender. Using the same skillet, melt remaining butter over high heat, add the chicken livers, and cook 4 to 5 minutes, turning frequently. The livers should be thoroughly browned outside, but still pink inside. (Slice one to check.) Add the livers and pan juices to the onions in the blender, then put in sherry, Calvados, cream, salt, pepper, and curry powder. Blend at high speed until the pâté is completely smooth. A narrow rubber spatula is helpful for this job. Taste the pâté and correct seasoning, if necessary. Place pâté in a crock and cover with plastic wrap to keep it from darkening. Refrigerate for at least 3 to 4 hours. Serve on lettuce leaves.

25.3 grams of carbohydrate in entire recipe; if serving 5, each serving contains 5.1 grams of carbohydrate.

1,578 calories in entire recipe; if serving 5, each serving contains 316 calories.

MELON WITH PROSCIUTTO

Makes 4 servings. A perennial favorite.

1 whole cantaloupe, about 5 inches in diameter
¼ pound Italian prosciutto, preferably imported (page 17)
Freshly ground black pepper
Lemon or lime wedges, if desired

Slice the cantaloupe into 8 wedges. Wrap a slice of the prosciutto around each piece. Place 2 wedges of the cantaloupe on each of four plates and serve with a pepper mill so that people can grind some fresh black pepper over their own servings. Lemon or lime wedges may be added to each plate, if desired.

28.0 grams of carbohydrate in entire recipe; if serving 4, each serving contains 7.0 grams of carbohydrate.
347 calories in entire recipe; if serving 4, each serving contains 85 calories.

NOTE: If cantaloupe is out of season, you may substitute any melon that is available.

RUMAKI

Makes 18 skewers. Polynesian Rumaki can be used as an appetizer to start a meal or as an hors d'oeuvre for a party.

½ pound bacon
½ pound chicken livers
2 tablespoons soy sauce
2 tablespoons dry sherry
1 tablespoon peanut oil
1 clove garlic, minced
Slice of fresh ginger root, minced
Artificial sweetener equal to 2 teaspoons sugar
9 water chestnuts, fresh or canned

Partially fry or broil the bacon, cut each piece in half, and set aside. Cut each chicken liver in half and remove any bits of tendon. Combine the soy sauce, sherry, oil, garlic, ginger, and artificial sweetener. Place the precooked bacon and the livers in the soy-sherry marinade for at least 30 minutes, or 1 hour if time is available. Slice each water chestnut in half. Wrap a piece of marinated chicken liver around a slice of water chestnut, then wrap a piece of bacon around the liver, and spear with a dampened toothpick or tiny skewer. Repeat until all pieces are wrapped and speared. Broil the Rumaki about 4 inches from the source of heat for 4 to 5 minutes, turning several times. The liver should remain pink inside. Serve hot.

25.3 grams of carbohydrate in entire recipe; makes 18 Rumaki, each one containing 1.4 grams of carbohydrate.

2,034 calories in entire recipe; makes 18 Rumaki, each one containing 113 calories.

CELERY AND MUSHROOMS WITH ROQUEFORT FILLING

Makes 1 cup filling

¼ pound imported French Roquefort cheese
¼ pound (1 stick) sweet butter
4 teaspoons Cognac
Few drops of Worcestershire sauce
Fresh mushrooms, all the same size
Minced fresh parsley
Fresh, crisp celery

Mash together thoroughly the cheese, butter, and Cognac. Stir in a few drops of Worcestershire sauce to taste. Wipe the mushrooms with a damp cloth. Remove the stems and save for future use. Fill the mushroom caps with the Roquefort mixture, then sprinkle the tops lightly with the parsley. Wash and dry the celery, cut into 2-inch pieces, and fill them with the cheese mixture. Sprinkle with parsley. Arrange mushrooms and celery in a decorative manner and serve as an appetizer or as part of an hors d'oeuvre tray.

2.4 grams of carbohydrate in filling recipe; makes 1 cup, each tablespoon containing 0.2 grams of carbohydrate. Add 0.5 grams of carbohydrate for each mushroom cap used and 2.0 grams of carbohydrate for each whole celery stalk.

872 calories in entire recipe; makes 1 cup, each tablespoon containing 55 calories. Add 4 calories for each mushroom cap used and 8 calories for each whole celery stalk.

SHRIMP COCKTAILS

Makes 6 servings

1½ pounds large raw shrimp, cleaned and deveined
1 cup water
½ cup dry white wine
1 small bay leaf
¼ teaspoon thyme
¾ teaspoon salt
4 peppercorns
Wedge of lemon
Any shrimp sauce recipe (see Chapter X)
6 medium-sized shells
Lettuce leaves

Place the shrimp in a saucepan with the water, wine, bay leaf, thyme, salt, and peppercorns. It's nice to tie the spices in a little cheesecloth and then add them to the pot. Cover the pan, bring to a boil, then lower the flame, and simmer for about 8 minutes. Do not overcook the shrimp. Remove shrimp from the liquid, drain thoroughly, and chill.

To serve, divide the shrimp among 6 seashells, each lined with a lettuce leaf. Spoon some of the sauce over each portion or serve sauce separately in another dish for dipping. Garnish with a wedge of lemon.

7.1 grams of carbohydrate in entire recipe; if serving 6, each serving contains 1.2 grams of carbohydrate plus the grams for your chosen sauce.
428 calories in entire recipe; if serving 6, each serving contains 71 calories plus the calories for your chosen sauce.

HOT SHRIMP COCKTAILS

Makes 6 servings. Try a change from the usual cold shrimp cocktail.

1½ pounds raw shrimp
1 cup water
½ cup dry white wine
1 small bay leaf
¼ teaspoon thyme
¾ teaspoon salt
4 peppercorns
1 large or 2 small cloves garlic, minced
6 tablespoons butter, melted
¼ cup imported Parmesan cheese
Salt and freshly ground black pepper to taste
6 medium-sized shells or ramekins
Minced parsley

Clean and devein shrimp, then place in a saucepan with water, wine, bay leaf, thyme, salt, and peppercorns. Cover pan, bring to a boil, and simmer for 6 to 7 minutes. Remove shrimp from the liquid and drain thoroughly. Preheat oven to 425° F. Distribute shrimp evenly among 6 shells or ramekins, then add the minced garlic to the melted butter, and spoon a tablespoonful over each serving. Sprinkle with Parmesan cheese, salt, and freshly ground pepper to taste, and bake in a 425° F. oven about 5 minutes. The butter should be sizzling. Sprinkle with minced parsley and serve immediately.

8.9 grams of carbohydrate in entire recipe; if serving 6, each serving contains 2.2 grams of carbohydrate.
1,145 calories in entire recipe; if serving 6, each serving contains 286 calories.

GRILLED TIDBIT

Serves 4. An unusual combination of ingredients, but they taste good together.

1 can skinless and boneless sardines
1 tablespoon minced onion
¼ teaspoon salt
⅛ teaspoon black pepper
½ teaspoon lemon juice
12 thin slices bacon

Drain the oil from the sardines. Place in a bowl and mash well with a fork. Add onion, salt, pepper, and lemon juice and mix well. Lay the bacon slices out on a board. Spread each one with some of the sardine mixture. Roll up the bacon slices like jelly rolls. Fasten with dampened, wooden toothpicks. Place on a broiler rack and broil until crisp. Serve hot.

3.6 grams of carbohydrate in entire recipe; makes 12 tidbits, each one containing 0.3 grams.
718 calories in entire recipe; makes 12 tidbits, each one containing 60 calories.

Reprinted from *A Treasury of Great Recipes* by Mary & Vincent Price.

CONSOMMÉ WITH SHERRY

Serves 4. Precede a heavy dinner with a light, delicately flavored broth.

4 cups beef broth, fresh, canned or made from a cube or powder
4–8 teaspoons dry sherry

Prepare beef broth as directed from the can or package mix you are using. Pour steaming hot broth into soup cups. To each cup, add 1 or 2 teaspoons dry sherry and stir. Serve very hot.

2.2 grams of carbohydrate in entire recipe; if serving 4, each serving contains 0.6 grams of carbohydrate.

97 calories in entire recipe; if serving 4, each serving contains 24 calories.

STRACCIATELLA SOUP

Serves 5. A popular Italian soup.

2 eggs
4 tablespoons freshly grated Parmesan cheese
4 cups chicken broth, fresh, canned, or made with a cube
4 tablespoons freshly minced parsley
Salt and freshly ground pepper to taste

Beat eggs thoroughly. Add cheese and a few tablespoons of unheated broth and beat together with the eggs. Heat remaining broth to boiling point, and add the egg-cheese mixture slowly, stirring constantly. Simmer the soup for about 5 minutes, stirring constantly. Remove from flame, stir in minced parsley, and ladle soup into hot bowls or soup cups. Additional cheese may be added, if desired.

3.4 grams of carbohydrate in entire recipe; if serving 5, each serving contains 0.7 grams of carbohydrate.

324 calories in entire recipe; if serving 5, each serving contains 65 calories.

GAZPACHO SOUP

Serves 6. This is really a soup salad.

3 very ripe tomatoes, peeled, seeded, and sliced
1 green pepper, seeded and sliced
1 medium cucumber, peeled, seeded, and sliced
½ onion, sliced
½ cup chilled beef broth
3 tablespoons wine vinegar
2 tablespoons olive oil
1 large clove garlic, minced
½ teaspoon basil
Salt and freshly ground pepper to taste—depends on degree of salt in
    broth
⅛ teaspoon ground celery seed
⅛–¼ teaspoon ground cumin

Place all ingredients in a blender and blend at moderate speed until vegetables are just chopped. Do not overblend. Chill thoroughly until time to serve. Serve in chilled cups or bowls. Add 1 or 2 ice cubes to each plate, if desired.

43.2 grams of carbohydrate in entire recipe; if serving 6, each serving contains 7.2 grams of carbohydrate.
423 calories in entire recipe; if serving 6, each serving contains 71 calories.

EASY BORSCHT

Makes 12 servings. Making borscht with canned beets is much easier than using fresh beets and tastes just as good.

One 1-pound can whole beets
2 quarts cold water
¼ teaspoon salt or more to taste

Artificial sweetener equal to 5 tablespoons sugar
4 eggs
Sour cream

Grate the canned beets, reserving the liquid from the can. Bring the water to a boil, add beets, beet liquid, and salt. Return to boil, then lower flame, and simmer 5 minutes. Remove from heat and stir in artificial sweetener. Beat the eggs thoroughly with a wire whisk. Add 1 cup of the hot liquid to eggs, whisking thoroughly as you pour, then whisk egg mixture thoroughly into the hot soup. Chill soup thoroughly. Serve with sour cream on the side and let people help themselves or add a dollop on top of each serving.

62.5 grams of carbohydrate in entire recipe; if serving 12, each serving contains 5.2 grams of carbohydrate. Add 0.5 grams of carbohydrate for each tablespoon of sour cream.
610 calories in entire recipe; if serving 12, each serving contains 51 calories. Add 29 calories for each tablespoon of sour cream.

FRESH MUSHROOM SOUP—HOT OR COLD

Makes 6 servings

1 pound fresh white mushrooms
2¼ cups double strength chicken broth
½ cup heavy cream
¼ cup dry sherry
Salt
Freshly ground pepper
Ground nutmeg
Minced parsley

Wipe the mushrooms with a damp paper towel and coarsely slice them. Place them in a blender container, add 1 cup of the chicken broth and purée the mixture. Pour it into the top of a double boiler or into a saucepan placed over a gentle heat. Add the remaining 1¼ cups of chicken broth, the heavy cream, and the dry sherry. Season with salt, pepper and nutmeg to taste. Bring the soup to a boil over low heat, then cover it with plastic wrap or aluminum foil to prevent a skin from forming over it.

This soup can be made in advance and reheated, but do not cook it further. Since this is a rich soup, it is best served in soup cups. Sprinkle the top with the minced parsley. This soup may also be chilled in the refrigerator and served cold. It's even better than Vichysoisse.

30.5 grams of carbohydrate in entire recipe; if serving 6, each serving contains 5.1 grams of carbohydrate.
841 calories in entire recipe; if serving 6, each serving contains 140 calories.

FRENCH ONION SOUP

Makes 8 servings. Did you ever eat onion soup at Les Halles in Paris at 4:00 A.M.? I was twenty-one when I took my first trip to Europe, supposedly to go to the Sorbonne, but I never even registered for the course. My happiest memory is eating a soup very like this one.

6 small onions
3 tablespoons butter
1 teaspoon flour
6 cups beef broth
½ cup very dry white wine or vermouth
1 tablespoon Cognac—optional
Salt to taste
Freshly ground black pepper to taste
3 tablespoons grated Swiss Emmenthal cheese
Additional grated Parmesan cheese

Slice the onions very thin. Sauté them in the butter until lightly browned. Mix in the flour and cook for 2 or 3 minutes more. Stir in the beef broth, wine, and Cognac. Season to taste with salt and freshly ground black pepper. Gently simmer the soup for 15 to 20 minutes. Add the Swiss cheese and continue simmering until the cheese melts. Stir frequently while the cheese melts. When serving, sprinkle each serving with additional grated Parmesan cheese.

34.8 grams of carbohydrate in entire recipe; if serving 8, each serving contains **4.6** grams of carbohydrate. Add **0.2** grams extra for each tablespoon of grated Parmesan used.

562 calories in entire recipe; if serving 8, each serving contains **70** calories. Add **25** calories extra for each tablespoon of grated Parmesan used.

BISQUE OF ZUCCHINI

Makes 4 servings.

1 pound zucchini, unpeeled
1 small onion, coarsely chopped
1 stalk celery, coarsely chopped
5 sprigs parsley
3 cups chicken broth, fresh, canned, or made with a cube
2 tablespoons heavy cream
2 tablespoons cold water
2 egg yolks
Salt and freshly ground pepper to taste

Wash zucchini thoroughly and chop coarsely without peeling. Place in a heavy saucepan with remaining vegetables and chicken broth. Bring the mixture to a boil and simmer uncovered for 40 minutes. Place the mixture in a blender and blend until smooth, then return it to the pot it was cooked in. Combine the egg yolks with the cream and water and a few tablespoons of the hot soup, then stir this mixture thoroughly into the soup. Reheat the soup if necessary, but do not allow it to boil. Add salt and pepper to taste.

24.9 grams of carbohydrate in entire recipe; if serving 4, each serving contains **6.2** grams of carbohydrate.

430 calories in entire recipe; if serving 4, each serving contains **108** calories.

FROTHY GREEK LEMON SOUP

Makes 6 servings. This light-as-air lemony soup is a delightful way to start a meal. Try it as a prelude to Shish Kebab.

4 cups chicken broth
4 extra-large eggs, at room temperature, separated
½ teaspoon cream of tartar
4 tablespoons lemon juice
6 thin slices of lemon

Bring the chicken broth to a boil. Meanwhile, beat the egg whites until foamy, add the cream of tartar, and continue beating until stiff but not dry. Beat the egg yolks with the lemon juice. Gently fold the egg whites into the yolks and gradually, with a wire whisk, stir in half of the boiling chicken broth. Immediately pour the mixture back into the remaining broth and continue heating over low heat, stirring constantly until thickened. Pour into soup cups and garnish with the thin slices of lemon.

10.8 grams of carbohydrate in entire recipe; if serving 6, each serving contains 1.8 grams of carbohydrate.
448 calories in entire recipe; if serving 6, each serving contains 75 calories.

COLD LEMON-SORREL SOUP

Makes 10 servings. This is a lemony version of the usual cold sorrel soup.

1 pound sorrel leaves
2 teaspoons salt
2 quarts water
¼ cup fresh lemon juice
Artificial sweetener equal to ¼ cup sugar
3 eggs
Sour cream

Trim the heavy stems from the sorrel, then wash and dry it. This is easily done by scrubbing your sink thoroughly and then filling it with cold water. Place the sorrel in the water and move it around with your hands. Change the water once or twice. Dry on paper towels or in a salad spinner. Shred the leaves and place in a heavy enamel saucepan with salt and water. Bring to a boil and cook for 20 minutes. Add lemon juice and cook 10 minutes more. Remove from heat and add artificial sweetener. Beat the eggs thoroughly with a wire whisk, then mix with 1 cup of the hot liquid, whisking thoroughly as you pour the liquid into the eggs. Whisk this egg mixture into the rest of the soup. Chill thoroughly. You can add sour cream to all of the soup beforehand, but I prefer to serve the sour cream on the side so people can help themselves or else to add a dollop on top of each serving.

24.1 grams of carbohydrate in entire recipe; if serving 10, each serving contains 2.4 grams of carbohydrate. Add 0.5 grams of carbohydrate for each tablespoon of sour cream.

387 calories in entire recipe; if serving 10, each serving contains 39 calories. Add 29 calories for each tablespoon of sour cream used.

CHILLED MELON SOUP

Makes 4 servings. For an appetizer or for dessert.

1½ pounds ripe cantaloupe, Spanish melon, or Casaba melon
2 tablespoons dry sherry
1½ teaspoons fresh lime juice
Artificial sweetener equal to 2 tablespoons sugar

Remove all seeds from the melon and trim away rind. Cut melon into small chunks and place in a blender. Add sherry, lime juice, and sweetener and blend until smooth. Pour the mixture into a plastic container or glass jar, cover, and refrigerate until very cold. Mix the soup thoroughly before putting into serving cups as it separates upon standing. To serve, garnish each soup cup with a sprig of fresh mint and 1 or 2 melon balls.

26.6 grams of carbohydrate in entire recipe; if serving 4, each serving contains 6.7 grams of carbohydrate.
150 calories in entire recipe; if serving 4, each serving contains 38 calories.

COLD FRESH RASPBERRY SOUP

Makes 6 servings. This sweet, delicious soup can be served as either an appetizer or as a dessert.

2 cups fresh raspberries
2 cups cold water
½ cup red wine
½ cup sour cream
Artificial sweetener equal to ½ cup sugar

Crush and strain the fresh raspberries. Mix in the water, wine, sour cream, and artificial sweetener. A wire whisk is good for this job. Chill thoroughly until serving time. Serve icy cold in chilled soup cups and garnish with 2 or 3 fresh raspberries and a sprig of fresh mint.

39.4 grams of carbohydrate in entire recipe; if serving 6, each serving contains 6.6 grams of carbohydrate.
471 calories in entire recipe; if serving 6, each serving contains 79 calories.

STRAWBERRY SOUP

Makes 6 servings. Again, serve as an appetizer or for dessert.

2 cups ripe strawberries
½ cup sour cream
2 cups cold water
½ cup Bordeaux or similar red wine
Artificial sweetener equal to ½ cup sugar

Wash and hull the strawberries, then place in a blender. Add sour cream and blend to a purée. Empty the mixture into a heavy saucepan and add water and wine. Heat the mixture very slowly over very low heat, stirring constantly with a wooden spoon. Do not let the soup boil. Remove from heat and stir in the artificial sweetener. Chill the soup, and when serving, garnish each plate with a few whole strawberries and a sprig of fresh mint.

28.6 grams of carbohydrate in entire recipe; if serving 6, each serving contains 4.8 grams of carbohydrate.
442 calories in entire recipe; if serving 6, each serving contains 74 calories.

IV.
MEATS: THE BACKBONE
OF LOW-CARBOHYDRATE
DIETS

Meats: The Backbone of Low-Carbohydrate Diets

Meats *are* the backbone of a low-carbohydrate diet because they contain *no* carbohydrates and are high in protein. At the same time, while steaks, roasts, hamburgers, and chops are delicious in themselves, one can become very bored eating them plain all the time. In this chapter, I have presented some low-carbohydrate variations on ways to prepare meats. Many of these recipes require very little more time and effort than just broiling a steak, yet they are interesting, tasty, and should keep anyone from becoming bored.

BEEF KEBABS

Makes 2 servings. Good for the barbecue, too.

1 pound sirloin steak
1 cup dry red wine
1 onion, chopped
1 carrot, chopped
2 shallots, chopped
6 peppercorns
Coarse salt
Pinch of thyme
1 bay leaf
3 cloves

2 tablespoons Cognac
12 medium-size mushroom caps
6 tiny, white onions, parboiled for 10 minutes
1 tablespoon melted butter

Cut meat into 2-inch cubes and marinate in a mixture of the wine, onion, carrot, shallots, peppercorns, salt, thyme, bay leaf, cloves, and Cognac. Allow meat to marinate 48 hours, turning the cubes occasionally, then drain, and dry each piece carefully in paper towels. Thread meat on skewers, alternating with mushroom caps and parboiled onions. Using a pastry brush, brush skewers with melted butter. Broil under a high flame, turning until meat is brown on all sides but still rare inside.

20.0 grams of carbohydrate in entire recipe; if serving 2, each serving contains 9.6 grams of carbohydrate.
916 calories in entire recipe; if serving 2, each serving contains 458 calories.

BEEF STROGANOFF

Makes 4 servings

1½ pounds fillet of beef
3 tablespoons butter
2 teaspoons olive oil
½ small onion, thinly sliced
4 medium-size fresh mushrooms, thinly sliced
⅓ cup dry white wine
1 cup sour cream
Salt
Freshly ground pepper
Dash of garlic powder
Dash of dry mustard
1 tablespoon and 1 teaspoon lemon juice
Few dashes of Worcestershire sauce
Minced parsley

Cut meat into very thin slices, or have butcher do it. Heat 2 table-spoons of the butter along with the oil in a large, heavy skillet. Get it as hot as possible, but do not let it burn. Sauté the beef slices in the hot fat very quickly—1 or 2 minutes per side. When delicately browned on both sides, remove to a hot platter. Add remaining butter to the skillet and sauté the onion slices until transparent. Add mushrooms, and sauté a few minutes longer. Add the wine and bring to a boil. Lower heat, add sour cream, salt, pepper, garlic powder, mustard, lemon juice, and Worcestershire sauce, and stir well. Heat the sauce over a low flame, warming it thoroughly, but do not allow it to boil as this would curdle the sour cream. Return meat to pan and warm the entire dish for about another minute. Sprinkle with fresh parsley as a garnish when serving.

17.9 grams of carbohydrate in entire recipe; if serving 4, each serving contains 4.5 grams of carbohydrate.

2,402 calories in entire recipe; if serving 4, each serving contains 601 calories.

FILLET OF BEEF IN VERMOUTH

Makes 4 servings. If you like olives, try this recipe.

2 tablespoons butter
Four 8-ounce fillets of beef, cut 1 inch thick
½ cup sliced green olives
¾ teaspoon salt
¼ teaspoon freshly ground black pepper
¼ cup dry vermouth
¼ cup heavy cream

Don't have any fat wrapped around the meat. Melt the butter in a skillet; add fillets and olives. Cook over high heat 2 minutes on each side, shaking the pan a few times. Sprinkle the meat with salt and pepper, add vermouth and cream. Cook over low heat 4 minutes longer, or to desired degree of rareness. Arrange fillets on a hot serving dish and pour sauce over them.

3.9 grams of carbohydrate in entire recipe; if serving 4, each serving contains 1.0 grams of carbohydrate.

2,499 calories in entire recipe; if serving 4, each serving contains .625 calories.

Reprinted with permission of Macmillan Publishing Co., Inc., from *The Pleasures of Italian Cooking* by Romeo Salta.

CHEESE-FILLED HAMBURGERS

Makes 4 servings. The lowly hamburger becomes a sophisticate.

2 pounds lean ground beef
Salt and freshly ground black pepper
Dash of garlic powder
4 tablespoons finely chopped onion
½ cup freshly chopped parsley
4 ounces French Roquefort cheese, crumbled
Strips of broiled bacon (optional)

Combine meat with salt, pepper, garlic powder, onion, and parsley. Shape meat into 4 elongated, flat hamburger patties, each about double the usual length. Sprinkle with crumbled Roquefort cheese. Fold each patty in half, shaping into 4 nice, fat hamburgers. Panbroil or broil to desired state of doneness. The cheese will melt throughout the meat and flavor it. Top with strips of broiled bacon, if desired.

6.0 grams of carbohydrate in entire recipe; if serving 4, each serving contains 1.5 grams of carbohydrate. Add 0.2 grams of carbohydrate for each thin slice of bacon.

2,068 calories in entire recipe; if serving 4, each serving contains 517 calories. Add 31 calories for each thin slice of bacon.

ITALIAN MEAT AND CHEESE CASSEROLE

Makes 4 servings. A delicious meal in one dish.

1 medium eggplant
3 tablespoons olive oil
2 teaspoons salt
½ teaspoon freshly ground black pepper
1 pound very lean ground beef
¼ pound chicken livers, diced
⅛ teaspoon garlic powder
¼ cup grated Parmesan cheese
6 ounces mozzarella cheese, thinly sliced
2 tablespoons butter

Preheat oven to 350° F. Peel eggplant and slice in thin slices. Place the oil in a heavy skillet and fry eggplant on both sides until golden brown. Sprinkle with 1 teaspoon of the salt and pepper. Sauté meat and diced chicken livers for 5 minutes, stirring constantly. Remove from heat and mix in 1 tablespoon of the Parmesan cheese, and remaining salt and pepper.

In a greased, pretty, 1-quart casserole, arrange a layer of eggplant, then a layer of meat, then a layer of mozzarella cheese. Repeat until all ingredients are used, ending with a layer of eggplant. Top with remaining Parmesan cheese and dot with butter. Bake at 350° F. for 1 hour. Serve immediately from the casserole.

22.9 grams of carbohydrate in entire recipe; if serving 4, each serving contains 5.7 grams of carbohydrate.

2,051 calories in entire recipe; if serving 4, each serving contains 513 calories.

MEAT-CRUSTED PIZZA

Makes 6 servings. Who needs a fattening bread crust on pizza anyway?

Crust:

1 pound very lean ground beef
1 egg
½ small onion, finely chopped
1 small clove garlic, finely chopped
1 teaspoon salt
¼ teaspoon black pepper
¼ teaspoon fennel seed

Filling:

¾ cup Italian plum tomatoes, drained and chopped
½ teaspoon crushed red pepper
¼ teaspoon oregano
¼ teaspoon basil
Salt and pepper to taste

Topping:

6 ounces mozzarella cheese
2 hot Italian sausages
¼ teaspoon oregano
3 tablespoons freshly grated Parmesan cheese

Mix together the beef, egg, onion, garlic, salt, black pepper, and fennel seed. Press the mixture into a 9-inch pie plate to form a shell. Preheat the oven to 375° F. Bake the pie shell 15 minutes, then pour off any fat that may have collected. If your meat was lean, you should have hardly any fat.

Mix together the tomatoes, red pepper, oregano, basil, and salt and pepper to taste. Spread the flavored tomatoes over the pie shell. Arrange the mozzarella in thin slices over the tomatoes. Cook the sausages 5 minutes, then drain, and slice into ½-inch rounds. Arrange sausage rounds over cheese. Sprinkle the pizza with another ¼ teaspoon of oregano, then with grated Parmesan cheese. You may add any other toppings you desire to this. Bake pizza for 15 minutes, then cut in 6 pie-shaped wedges and serve piping hot.

19.0 grams of carbohydrate in entire recipe; if serving 6, each serving contains 3.3 grams of carbohydrate.

1,965 calories in entire recipe; if serving 6, each serving contains 328 calories.

LONDON BROIL WITH BOURSIN

Makes 4 servings. This is one of the easiest recipes in this book. It's become a favorite of many of my friends.

One 5-ounce package French Boursin cheese with herbs
One 2-pound piece London Broil, cut from the round
Salt
Freshly ground pepper

Bring the Boursin to room temperature by allowing it to stand out of the refrigerator for about 2 hours until very soft. Sprinkle the London Broil with salt and pepper to taste. Place meat in a preheated broiler and broil for approximately 5 minutes on each side under very high heat. The outside should be browned and the inside rare for the meat to be tender. Remove meat to a large platter and slice diagonally into very thin slices. Pass the softened Boursin separately as a dipping sauce for the meat.

5.0 grams of carbohydrate in entire recipe; if serving 4, each serving contains 1.3 grams of carbohydrate.

2,288 calories in entire recipe; if serving 4, each serving contains 572 calories.

NOTE: You may substitute 4–8-ounce boneless steaks grilled to your taste for the London Broil.

SOY-GLAZED LONDON BROIL

Makes 3 servings. Would you have ever thought of making London Broil Chinese style?

1 flank steak, weighing about 1½ pounds
2 tablespoons soy sauce
2 tablespoons dry sherry or saké
1 tablespoon peanut oil
Few drops Tabasco
1½ cloves fresh garlic, minced
2 slices fresh ginger root, finely minced

Marinate the steak overnight in a mixture of the soy sauce, sherry, oil, Tabasco, garlic and ginger root. This can be done in a large bowl or better still in a plastic bag. Turn the meat occasionally in the marinade to flavor all parts. Preheat your broiler for at least 10 minutes, then broil the meat 3 inches from the flame for approximately 3 minutes on each side, basting with the marinade. Flank steak must be served rare to keep it from becoming tough. If you don't like rare meat, buy another cut of meat for this recipe. To serve, carve the meat at a diagonal, using a 45° angle, into thin slices. Overlap the slices on a heated serving dish and pour the pan juices over them.

6.0 grams of carbohydrate in entire recipe; if serving 3, each serving contains 2.0 grams of carbohydrate.

1,046 calories in entire recipe; if serving 3, each serving contains 349 calories.

ROQUEFORT-TOPPED STEAK

Makes 4 servings. Feeling lazy? Don't want to do more than just broil a steak? This takes only 1 minute more.

2 pounds lean, boneless steak, cut in 4 portions
Salt
Freshly ground pepper
Garlic powder
2 ounces French Roquefort cheese
4 teaspoons Chablis or other very dry white wine
15 drops Cognac extract (page 16) or any good brandy extract
4 teaspoons olive oil

Sprinkle steak to taste with salt, pepper, and garlic powder. Broil to desired state of doneness. While steak is broiling, mix together Roquefort cheese, wine, extract, and oil. When steak is done to taste, top with Roquefort mixture, and broil 1 or 2 minutes longer until topping melts. Remove from broiler and pour pan juices over steak.

1.0 grams of carbohydrate in entire recipe; if serving 4, each serving contains 0.3 grams of carbohydrate.

2,350 calories in entire recipe; if serving 4, each serving contains 588 calories.

STEAK WITH CHICKEN-LIVER SAUCE

Makes 4 servings. An elegant dinner!

2 tablespoons butter
1 large clove of garlic, minced
2 shallots, minced
½ pound chicken livers
1 bay leaf
½ teaspoon salt

Generous sprinkling of freshly ground black pepper
¼ teaspoon sage
¼ teaspoon thyme
½ cup beef stock (may be made with a bouillon cube)
2 teaspoons dry sherry
½ teaspoon Madras curry powder (page 15)
Four ½-pound lean, boneless beef steaks

Heat the butter in a skillet. Add the garlic, shallots, chicken livers, and bay leaf and sauté 3 minutes over high heat. Add salt, pepper, sage, and thyme and sauté 2 minutes more. Discard bay leaf and place liver mixture in a blender. Add beef stock, sherry, and curry powder and blend until smooth. Keep warm over a very low flame.

Heat the remaining butter until it sizzles, add steaks and brown quickly over high heat to the desired doneness. Place steaks on a serving dish, pour chicken-liver sauce over them, and serve.

8.0 grams of carbohydrate in entire recipe; if serving 4, each serving contains 2.0 grams of carbohydrate.

2,480 calories in entire recipe; if serving 4, each serving contains 620 calories.

STEAK MOUTARDE FLAMBÉ

Makes 4 servings. Even if you've always believed that a steak needs only to be broiled, try this. You might change your mind.

1 tablespoon butter
Four ½-pound fillets of beef, 1½ inches thick
Salt
Coarsely ground pepper
¼ teaspoon rosemary
½ teaspoon sage
¼ cup Cognac
4 teaspoons Dijon-style mustard
4 teaspoons mild mustard

¼ teaspoon paprika
2 tablespoons sour cream
¼ cup heavy sweet cream

Heat the butter in a skillet. Sauté the fillets 4 minutes over high heat. Turn and sprinkle with salt, pepper, rosemary, and sage and cook 4 minutes more. Pour off any excess fat from pan and sprinkle fillets with Cognac. Ignite the Cognac and when flame burns out, transfer fillets to a warm serving platter, and keep warm. To the skillet, add the mustards and paprika, then combine sour cream and sweet cream, and add, stirring well. Cook, still stirring, for 1 minute. Pour sauce over fillets and serve.

6.7 grams of carbohydrate in entire recipe; if serving 4, each serving contains 1.4 grams of carbohydrate.

2,533 calories in entire recipe; if serving 4, each serving contains 633 calories.

Reprinted from *A Treasury of Great Recipes* by Mary & Vincent Price.

STEAK WITH MUSHROOM SAUCE

Makes 4 servings

3 tablespoons lemon juice
4 shell steaks, about 8 ounces each
Salt and freshly ground pepper
1 teaspoon bacon drippings
2 tablespoons finely chopped shallots
¼ pound mushrooms, thinly sliced
½ clove garlic, finely minced
½ cup dry red wine
1 teaspoon meat extract, such as Bovril
½ bay leaf
1 teaspoon flour

1 teaspoon butter
1 tablespoon dry red wine
Chopped parsley

Pour lemon juice over steaks and let marinate for about 10 minutes. Drain. Sprinkle with salt and pepper. Heat bacon drippings until lightly browned. Add mushrooms and garlic, and sauté for a few minutes more. Add the wine, meat extract, and bay leaf, bring to a boil, and simmer 5 minutes. Put steaks in the gravy, heat 3 minutes, then place on a preheated platter. Keep warm. Thicken gravy with the flour and butter which have been mixed together and thinned with 1 tablespoon wine. Pour a little gravy over steaks and sprinkle with fresh parsley. Serve remaining gravy on the side.

13.7 grams of carbohydrate in entire recipe; if serving 4, each serving contains 3.4 grams of carbohydrate.

3,413 calories in entire recipe; if serving 4, each serving contains 853 calories.

Reprinted from *Annemarie's Personal Cookbook* by Annemarie Huste.

VEAL SCALLOPS WITH CHIVES AND CHEESE

Makes 6 servings. Veal and cheese are always a good combination.

2 pounds veal scallops, pounded flat
Salt
Freshly ground pepper
2 tablespoons butter
2 teaspoons olive oil
1 cup dry white wine
½ cup heavy cream
2 tablespoons chives, fresh, frozen, or freeze-dried
6 ounces Swiss Gruyère cheese (page 13), thinly sliced

Salt and pepper the veal scallops. Melt 2 tablespoons of butter in a large skillet, or 2 smaller ones. Add 2 teaspoons olive oil to keep butter from burning. Sauté veal scallops in a single layer about 5 minutes on each side, or until well browned. Remove to a baking dish large enough to hold the veal in a single layer. Deglaze pan or pans with 1 cup dry white wine, scraping up all browned bits from pan bottom. Cook down until liquid is reduced by half the original volume. Add the cream and chives and boil for 2 minutes more or until sauce thickens. Pour the sauce over the veal, top with sliced cheese, and place under broiler. Broil until the cheese melts.

8.8 grams of carbohydrate in entire recipe; if serving 6, each serving contains 1.5 grams of carbohydrate.

3,156 calories in entire recipe; if serving 6, each serving contains 526 calories.

PARTY VEAL SCALLOPS

Makes 4 servings

1 pound veal scallops, pounded thin
1 tablespoon butter
½ tablespoon good quality olive oil
1 cup grated Swiss Gruyère cheese (page 13)
½ cup heavy cream
2 scant teaspoons Dijon-style mustard
½ cup dry white wine
Salt
Generous amount of freshly ground black pepper

Sauté the veal scallops on both sides in a mixture of the butter and oil. The oil will keep the butter from burning. Meanwhile, combine Gruyère cheese, cream, and mustard. Remove the veal scallops to a heatproof, shallow oven dish. Deglaze the pan used for the scallops with wine, scraping up any browned bits. Boil a few minutes to evaporate all alcohol. Pour the wine over the scallops, top with cheese mixture, and place under the broiler until cheese browns. Serve immediately while hot.

7.1 grams of carbohydrate in entire recipe; if serving 4, each serving contains 1.8 grams of carbohydrate.

1,817 calories in entire recipe; if serving 4, each serving contains 454 calories.

VEAL CHOPS IN MUSTARD SAUCE

Makes 4 servings. One of the more delicious ways of preparing veal chops. Fast, too.

1 tablespoon butter
4 thick, lean rib veal chops, each weighing approximately 8 ounces
2 teaspoons softened butter
2 tablespoons wine vinegar
1½ teaspoons Dijon-style mustard
3 tablespoons heavy sweet cream
2 tablespoons olive oil
½ teaspoon salt
¼ teaspoon freshly ground black pepper
4 tablespoons finely chopped fresh parsley

Melt the butter in a heavy, Teflon-coated skillet. Add the chops to the skillet and cook them over medium heat for approximately 10 minutes on each side or till done. In a tiny saucepan, heat the next 7 ingredients together, stirring frequently. Do not boil the mixture. When the chops are cooked, remove them to a heated platter. Pour off any excess fat that may have accumulated in the skillet and add the mustard mixture to the pan. Heat over a low flame to combine the mustard mixture with the pan juices. Pour the sauce over the chops and garnish with chopped parsley.

3.8 grams of carbohydrate in entire recipe; if serving 4, each serving contains 1.0 grams of carbohydrate.

1,803 calories in entire recipe; if serving 4, each serving contains 451 calories.

LAMB SHISH KEBAB

Makes 2 servings. This recipe was given to me by one of the women I once worked with. I can no longer remember her name, but I've never forgotten her delicious recipe.

¼ cup olive oil
¼ cup dry white wine
2 tablespoons grated onion
½ teaspoon garlic powder
½ teaspoon salt
½ teaspoon freshly grated black pepper
1 teaspoon caraway seeds
1 teaspoon oregano
1 pound lean, boneless lamb
1 medium green pepper, cut in 8 pieces
6 tiny, white onions, parboiled for 10 minutes
1 small tomato, quartered
4 medium mushroom caps

Combine the oil, wine, onion, garlic powder, salt, pepper, caraway seeds, and oregano in a bowl. Cut the lamb into 1½-inch cubes and add to the marinade. Stir the lamb in the marinade until it is thoroughly coated. Marinate the meat at least 24 hours or longer, if you prefer, turning the cubes occasionally. Thread the meat on skewers, alternating with the green pepper, white onions, tomato, and mushroom caps. Broil under a high flame, turning the skewers until the meat is brown on all sides but still pink inside. Lamb tastes better when it is not too well done. Baste occasionally with the marinade while broiling. Serve hot.

22.2 grams of carbohydrate in entire recipe; if serving 2, each serving contains 11.1 grams of carbohydrate.

1,547 calories in entire recipe; if serving 2, each serving contains 774 calories.

SAUTÉED CALF'S LIVER

Makes 4 servings

30 grams (¼ cup, unsifted) full-fat soy flour
½ teaspoon salt
2 dashes garlic powder
2 dashes ground celery seed
¼ teaspoon freshly ground black pepper
2 pounds calf's liver, sliced ⅜–½ inch thick
4 tablespoons butter
1 cup dry white wine
2 tablespoons freshly chopped chives
Parsley for garnish

Combine the soy flour with the salt, garlic powder, onion powder, celery seed, and black pepper. Dredge the liver in seasoned soy flour and shake off excess flour. Heat the butter in a large, heavy skillet, arrange the liver in a single layer, and sauté 2 to 3 minutes, regulating the flame so the butter is always very hot but not burning. Turn liver and sauté for 1 or 2 minutes more. The liver is done when it is just a pale pink inside. Remove to a hot platter and add the wine to the skillet. Over a high flame, deglaze the pans, scraping up any browned bits. Cook briefly until the alcohol smell has completely disappeared. Add chopped chives and cook another minute. Pour the sauce over the liver, decorate platter with parsley sprigs, and serve hot.

47.0 grams of carbohydrate in entire recipe; if serving 4, each serving contains 12.0 grams of carbohydrate.
1,964 calories in entire recipe; if serving 4, each serving contains 491 calories.

NOTE: When purchasing the liver, ask the butcher to remove the surrounding filament from each slice of liver. If filament is left on, the liver will curl as it cooks.

SAUTÉED HAM SLICES IN CHERRY SAUCE

Makes 4 servings

1 jar sugarless cherry jam
2 tablespoons dry sherry
A dash of ground cloves
Artificial sweetener equal to 6 tablespoons sugar
2 slices cooked, lean ham (¾ pound each)
1 tablespoon butter
Watercress or parsley for garnish

In a heavy saucepan, heat the jam with the sherry and cloves. Bring to a boil and boil 2 minutes. Remove from the heat and add artificial sweetener. Allow the sauce to sit off the heat long enough to thicken slightly. Meanwhile, slash the edges of the ham slices to keep them from curling up. In a heavy skillet, brown the slices in butter for 8 minutes on each side. Remove to a warm serving platter and spoon some of the sauce over the ham. Garnish the platter with parsley or watercress for a pretty color contrast.

4.5 grams of carbohydrate in entire recipe; if serving 4, each serving contains 1.1 grams of carbohydrate.

2,098 calories in entire recipe; if serving 4, each serving contains 525 calories.

V.
FISH: GIFTS
FROM THE SEA

Fish: Gifts from the Sea

I think the reason most people don't like fish is that the fish we get in supermarkets is not fresh enough. When really fresh, fish has neither a fishy smell nor a fishy taste. It is delicate and delicious! Things to look for when buying fresh fish are bright sparkling eyes, flesh that springs back when pressed, and no fishy smell.

BROILED BLUEFISH WITH BACON

Makes 2 servings. The bacon on this may even please a fish-hater.

One 2¼–2½-pound bluefish, filleted (1 pound of fillets)
Garlic powder
Freshly ground pepper
2 thick slices bacon
Minced parsley
Lemon slices

Make individual trays for each serving out of double-weight aluminum foil because it is very difficult to remove the fish without ruining the way it looks. Place each serving of fish on its own tray and sprinkle lightly with garlic powder and pepper. Place a strip of bacon on each piece and broil until fish flakes easily when tested with a fork, basting frequently with bacon drippings. If bacon gets crisp before fish is ready, remove to a warm platter and keep warm.

When the fish tests done, remove it, foil and all, to a serving platter. Sprinkle each serving with freshly minced parsley, place a lemon slice alongside, and top with a crisp slice of bacon. Serve fish hot in its own tray. Coleslaw makes a nice accompaniment.

1.9 grams of carbohydrate in entire recipe; if serving 2, each serving contains 1.0 grams of carbohydrate.
611 calories in entire recipe; if serving 2, each serving contains 306 calories.

MUSTARD-FLAVORED SPANISH MACKEREL

Makes 4 servings

4 tablespoons butter
2 tablespoons Dijon-style mustard
¼ cup fresh lemon juice
Spanish mackerel fillets weighing about 2 pounds
Salt
Freshly ground black pepper
2 tablespoons fresh dill, finely chopped

Melt the butter in a tiny saucepan. Mix in the mustard and the lemon juice. Wash and dry the fillets, then sprinkle them to taste with salt and freshly ground black pepper. Arrange the fillets on aluminum foil, skin-side down. Baste the fish with approximately ½ of the mustard-butter and broil it for a few minutes. Baste the fish with the remaining mustard-butter and continue to broil until the fish flakes easily when tested with a fork. Sprinkle with the chopped dill and serve immediately.

8.2 grams of carbohydrate in entire recipe; if serving 4, each serving contains 2.1 grams of carbohydrate.
2,084 calories in entire recipe; if serving 4, each serving contains 521 calories.

GRILLED SALMON STEAKS WITH ANCHOVY BUTTER

Makes 4 servings. Anchovy butter is the perfect accent for grilled salmon.

¼ pound (1 stick) unsalted butter, softened
Four 8-ounce slices fresh salmon steak
1 teaspoon tarragon
Salt
Freshly ground black pepper
1 tablespoon anchovy paste

Melt 2 tablespoons of the butter and add tarragon to it. Brush salmon steaks with half the melted butter, then sprinkle very lightly with salt and pepper. Place in a preheated broiler and broil until one side is golden brown. Turn the fish, brush with remaining butter, and broil second side until it is golden brown and fish flakes easily when tested with a fork.

While the salmon is broiling, make anchovy butter by creaming together the remaining softened butter with the anchovy paste. Shape the mixture into pats, circles, or rosettes and refrigerate until salmon is ready. Remove salmon steaks to a warm platter and top each piece with anchovy butter.

1.8 grams of carbohydrate in entire recipe; if serving 4, each serving contains 0.5 grams of carbohydrate.

2,116 calories in entire recipe; if serving 4, each serving contains 529 calories.

SHAD EN PAPILLOTE

Makes 4 servings. This is the nicest way I've ever found to prepare fish.

2 pounds shad fillets, cut in 4 pieces
4 teaspoons dry white wine
4 tablespoons heavy cream
Garlic powder
Salt
Freshly ground black pepper
4 tablespoons freshly grated Parmesan cheese
Lemon wedges
Parsley

Preheat oven to 425° F. Make 4 casings of aluminum foil large enough to hold each piece of fish with room to make a double fold at the edges. The foil may be cut like a large folded heart or a folded rectangle. (To make a heart, take each piece of aluminum foil, fold it in half to double it, and cut out a large heart that is joined at the bottom where you have folded it.)

Place 1 shad fillet piece in the center of each foil casing and sprinkle with a teaspoon of wine. Add 1 tablespoon of cream to each fillet, then sprinkle lightly with garlic powder, salt, pepper and 1 tablespoon of Parmesan cheese. Seal the foil packages tightly by folding both edges together twice. Bake in the preheated oven for 20 minutes, at which time the fish should be done, flaking easily when tested with a fork. Serve in the foil. It looks very impressive, particularly if you have made the hearts. Decorate each plate with lemon wedges and fresh parsley.

2.6 grams of carbohydrate in entire recipe; if serving 4, each serving contains 0.8 grams of carbohydrate.

1,895 calories in entire recipe; if serving 4, each serving contains 474 calories.

NOTE: If shad is not available, try this method with other white-meated fish.

SOLE CORDON BLEU

Makes 4 servings

4 fillets of sole, 8 ounces each
½ cup dry white wine
Salt
Pepper
Garlic powder
Dried dill weed
4 teaspoons butter
¼ pound boiled ham, cut into 4 slices
¼ pound Swiss cheese, preferably imported, cut into 4 slices

Wash and dry fillets, and arrange them in a shallow baking dish. Pour 1 tablespoon of wine over each fillet, then salt and pepper, and sprinkle lightly with garlic powder and dill. Dot with 2 teaspoons of the butter. Broil until fish just begins to acquire color (if browned, it will get too dry). With a pancake turner, turn the fillets over carefully without breaking them. Pour 1 tablespoon of remaining wine over each piece, then sprinkle again lightly with salt, pepper, garlic powder, and dill. Dot with the remaining butter, and broil until golden. Baste continually during the broiling on both sides with the wine drippings in the pan.

When fish is golden, cover each fillet with a ham slice and broil 1 or 2 minutes to warm the ham. Then cover each with a cheese slice and allow to broil until cheese melts (about 2 minutes more). Remove fish to warmed plates and pour any pan drippings over it. Garnish with sprigs of fresh parsley.

3.2 grams of carbohydrate in entire recipe; if serving 4, each serving contains 0.8 grams of carbohydrate.

1,616 calories in entire recipe; if serving 4, each serving contains 404 calories.

FILLET OF SOLE IN WHITE WINE

Makes 4 servings. This is truly the best fish recipe I have ever found. It can turn a fish hater into a fish eater.

Four 8-ounce fillets of sole
1¼ teaspoons salt
½ teaspoon white pepper
2 green onions or scallions, chopped
4 tablespoons (½ stick) melted butter
½ cup dry white wine
1 tablespoon chopped parsley
½ teaspoon thyme
2 bay leaves, crushed
1 tablespoon butter
1½ teaspoons flour
2 tablespoons heavy cream

Preheat oven to 375° F. Wash and dry fillets and season with salt and pepper. Arrange fillets in a buttered baking dish in a single layer and sprinkle with the green onions, melted butter, wine, parsley, thyme, and bay leaves. Cover with greased paper facing down, then cover dish, and bake 20 minutes. Carefully remove fillets from baking dish. Strain pan juices into a small saucepan, add 1 tablespoon butter, and let melt. Blend in the flour, add the cream, and cook 4 minutes. Pour over fish and serve.

6.2 grams of carbohydrate in entire recipe; if serving 4, each serving contains 1.6 grams of carbohydrate.

1,440 calories in entire recipe; if serving 4, each serving contains 360 calories.

Reprinted with permission of Macmillan Publishing Co., Inc., from *The Pleasures of Italian Cooking* by Romeo Salta.

FILLET OF SOLE WITH PARMESAN CHEESE

Serves 4. Would you like a quick fish meal?

Four 8-ounce fillets of sole
1 teaspoon salt
¼ teaspoon freshly ground black pepper
Dash of garlic powder
4 tablespoons butter
½ cup freshly grated Parmesan cheese
¼ cup bottled clam juice

Wash and dry the fillets. Season to taste with salt, garlic powder, and pepper. Melt 2 tablespoons of the butter in a Teflon-lined skillet and sauté the fish in it until golden brown on both sides. Sprinkle with cheese and the clam juice. Dot with the remaining butter. Cover the pan and cook over low heat for another 5 minutes.

3.0 grams of carbohydrate in entire recipe; if serving 4, each serving contains 0.8 grams of carbohydrate.
1,347 calories in entire recipe; if serving 4, each serving contains 337 calories.

SCAMPI

Makes 6 appetizer servings or 3 main dish servings. Italy's gift to the diet world!

1½ pounds very large fresh shrimp in the shell
4 tablespoons (½ stick) butter, melted
2 tablespoons Italian olive oil
2 large or 4 small cloves garlic, finely minced
1 teaspoon salt

Freshly ground black pepper
4 tablespoons finely chopped parsley
Lemon wedges

Shell the shrimp, or have it done, making sure the last quarter inch of shell (the tail) is left on. Slit the shrimp down the back and lift out black veins. Wash shrimp with cold water and dry with paper towels.

Combine the melted butter, olive oil, garlic, salt, and pepper, and marinate the shrimp in this mixture 1 to 2 hours. (Don't worry if the butter coagulates as it gets cold; it will melt again during broiling.)

Preheat the broiler. Place shrimp in a shallow, flameproof baking dish or in individual dishes and pour the marinade over it. Broil the shrimp 3 to 4 inches from the heat for 5 minutes. Turn them over and broil 5 to 10 minutes more until lightly browned and firm to the touch. Baste frequently while broiling. (Do not overcook!) Sprinkle with minced parsley and garnish with lemon wedges. Serve very hot.

8.3 grams of carbohydrate in entire recipe; if serving 6 as an appetizer, each serving contains 1.4 grams of carbohydrate; if serving 3 as a main dish, each serving contains 2.8 grams of carbohydrate.

955 calories in entire recipe; if serving 6 as an appetizer, each serving contains 159 calories; if serving 3 as a main dish, each serving contains 318 calories.

CURRIED SHRIMP SALAD

Makes 4 servings. An interesting version of shrimp salad.

2 cups cooked, cleaned tiny shrimp
1 cup diced celery
½ cup sugarless mayonnaise
1½–2 teaspoons Madras curry powder (page 15)
Dash of garlic powder

Salt
Freshly ground pepper to taste
Cantaloupe wedges

If only large shrimp are available, dice them. Mix together the cooked shrimp, celery, mayonnaise, curry powder, garlic powder, salt, and pepper. Chill until serving time. To serve, arrange a scoop of shrimp salad on a lettuce leaf and garnish with a wedge of cantaloupe.

10.8 grams of carbohydrate in entire recipe; if serving 4, each serving contains 2.7 grams of carbohydrate.
1,287 calories in entire recipe; if serving 4, each serving contains 322 calories.

BROILED LOBSTER TAILS

Makes 4 servings. An expensive treat, but an absolutely delicious dinner.

4 large lobster tails, about 12 ounces each
6 tablespoons (¾ stick) butter, melted
1 large lemon, cut in 4 wedges

Have the fishmonger split the lobster tails down the middle and clean them. Brush them with a little of the melted butter and broil for 12 to 18 minutes, brushing frequently with melted butter. When done, the tails will be golden brown and the lobster meat will come away from the shell. (Do not overcook!) Divide the remaining butter into 4 small dishes. Serve a dish of melted butter for dipping the lobster meat on the same plate as you serve the lobster tail. Add a lemon wedge to the plate so that the lemon juice may be squeezed into the butter.

7.8 grams of carbohydrate in entire recipe; if serving 4, each serving contains 2.0 grams of carbohydrate.
1,446 calories in entire recipe; if serving 4, each serving contains 362 calories.

SEAFOOD KEBABS

Makes 2-3 servings

4 tablespoons olive oil
2 tablespoons dry vermouth
Salt
Freshly ground black pepper
6 ounces fresh lobster meat, cut into 1½-inch cubes
6 ounces fresh scallops, halved crosswise
6 ounces fresh shrimp, cleaned and deveined (8 ounces before
    cleaning)
8 medium-sized fresh mushroom caps
1 medium tomato, cut in 8ths
1 green pepper, cut in 8ths
8 tiny white onions, parboiled 10 minutes

Mix together in a large bowl the oil, vermouth, salt and pepper. Place the lobster meat, scallops and shrimp in the oil mixture and stir to coat thoroughly. Cover with aluminum foil and refrigerate overnight.

Preheat the broiler for 15 minutes. Arrange the seafood on skewers, alternating the seafood with the vegetables. Broil for 12 to 18 minutes, depending on your broiler, until done, basting frequently with the marinade. Do not overcook.

43.0 grams of carbohydrate in entire recipe; if serving 3, each serving contains 14.3 grams of carbohydrate.
1,086 calories in entire recipe; if serving 3, each serving contains 362 calories.

VI.
CHICKEN: A DIETER'S BEST FRIEND

Chicken: A Dieter's Best Friend

Chicken is excellent for low-carbohydrate diets because not only is it low in carbohydrates and calories, it is also one of our most versatile foods. It is relatively inexpensive, combines well with many seasonings, and is delicious in salads, dressed up in its Sunday best, or just simply roasted or broiled with no trimmings!

CHICKEN BEAUVAIS

Makes 4 servings

One 3-pound frying chicken, cut in half
2 tablespoons butter
4 thin slices lemon
2 tablespoons dry sherry
½ cup heavy cream
4 thin 2-ounce slices Gruyère cheese
Salt and pepper to taste

Place chicken, skin side up, in a shallow roasting pan. Dot with butter and bake in a preheated 350° F. oven, placing pan near top of

138

oven, for about 30 minutes. Place 2 slices of lemon on each half of chicken. Mix together the sherry and cream and pour over the chicken. Cook 1 hour longer or until chicken is tender and crisp. Remove lemon slices and place 2 slices of cheese over each half of chicken. Bake until cheese melts. A little chicken broth may be added to pan if juices begin to evaporate. Remove chicken to a heated serving platter. Add salt and pepper to the juices in the pan and pour over the chicken.

11.9 grams of carbohydrate in entire recipe; if serving 4, each serving contains 3.0 grams of carbohydrate.

2,706 calories in entire recipe; if serving 4, each serving contains 677 calories.

NOTE: I usually prefer to have the chicken cut in quarters, then place a slice of lemon and a slice of cheese on each quarter. Also, if the juices begin to evaporate and chicken broth needs to be added, I like to add an extra bit of sherry to the broth first.

Recipe for Chicken Beauvais appeared in *The White House Chef Cookbook* by Rene Verdon.

CHICKEN ROQUEFORT

Makes 4 servings

One 3-pound chicken, cut in serving pieces
4 tablespoons (½ stick) butter, melted
1 cup sour cream
¼ cup crumbled Roquefort cheese
1 teaspoon Worcestershire sauce
Paprika

Brown chicken in butter. Mix sour cream, Roquefort cheese, and Worcestershire sauce and pour over chicken in a casserole. Sprinkle with paprika and bake in a preheated oven at 325° F. for about 30 minutes.

8.6 grams of carbohydrate in entire recipe; if serving 4, each serving contains 2.2 grams of carbohydrate.

2,117 calories in entire recipe; if serving 4, each serving contains 529 calories.

NOTE: I generally like to buy 3 large whole chicken breasts, each weighing about 1 pound and have them split to make 6 pieces.

Recipe for Chicken Roquefort appeared in *The White House Chef Cookbook* by Rene Verdon.

BROILED CHICKEN WITH SHALLOT BUTTER

Makes 2 servings. A delicate way of preparing chicken and a favorite of anyone who has tried it.

2 chicken breasts, each weighing about 1 pound, halved
6 tablespoons minced shallots
4 tablespoons (½ stick) butter
Salt
Freshly ground black pepper

Let the butter stand out for 10 to 15 minutes to soften a little. Combine the minced shallots with the softened butter. Divide the shallot butter into 4 equal parts and push one part under the skin of each quarter of chicken. Sprinkle the chicken breasts with salt and freshly ground black pepper to taste. Place the chicken breasts, skin side down, in a broiling pan. Broil the chicken breasts for 13 to 15 minutes. Turn the breasts over, skin side up, and broil them for 13 to 15 minutes more or till done. Baste them frequently with the shallot-flavored butter that has seeped out from under the skin. Remove to a heated serving platter and pour the shallot-flavored drippings over the chicken breasts.

7.2 grams of carbohydrate in entire recipe; if serving 2, each serving contains 3.6 grams of carbohydrate.

1,153 calories in entire recipe; if serving 2, each serving contains 577 calories.

MUSTARD BROILED CHICKEN

Makes 4 servings. Here's a chicken recipe for the mustard lovers.

4 whole chicken breasts (about 1 pound each), halved
½ cup Italian olive oil
3 tablespoons brown mustard
Salt
Freshly ground black pepper
Lemon wedges

Arrange the chicken breasts, skin-side down, on aluminum foil or on a broiling pan. Add the oil to the mustard slowly, beating with a fork to the consistency of mayonnaise. Brush the underside of chicken breasts with about a third of the mustard mixture. Broil 13 to 15 minutes. Turn chicken skin-side up, spread with remaining mustard mixture, and broil 13 to 15 minutes more, basting frequently with pan drippings. Sprinkle with salt and freshly ground pepper to taste and serve a lemon wedge alongside each portion of chicken.

4.5 grams of carbohydrate in entire recipe; if serving 4, each serving contains 1.1 grams of carbohydrate.

2,576 calories in entire recipe; if serving 4, each serving contains 644 calories.

CHICKEN IN BLUE CHEESE SAUCE

Makes 4 servings. An unusual combination of flavors that blend well together. The liquid smoke adds a high note.

1 cup cottage cheese
2 ounces blue cheese
¼ cup chopped parsley
¼ cup butter, softened
½ teaspoon salt
1 small clove garlic, crushed
¼ cup cold water
2 teaspoons liquid smoke
4 whole chicken breasts (about 1 pound each), halved

Combine cottage cheese, blue cheese, parsley, butter, salt, garlic, water, and liquid smoke in a blender until smooth. This will make a lovely green-colored sauce.

Wash and dry chicken breasts. Arrange them skin-side down on heavy duty aluminum foil or on a broiling pan. Spread about a third of the cheese mixture over the chicken and broil 13 to 15 minutes. Turn chicken breasts skin-side up and spread remaining cheese mixture on the skin. Broil another 13 to 15 minutes, basting occasionally with pan drippings. Serve hot.

8.6 grams of carbohydrate in entire recipe; if serving 4, each serving contains 2.2 grams of carbohydrate.

2,442 calories in entire recipe; if serving 4, each serving contains 611 calories.

BROILED CHICKEN AUX FINES HERBES

Makes 4 servings. A *fines herbes* mixture is just as good with chicken as it is with eggs.

¼ pound (1 stick) softened butter
½ cup chopped chives, fresh or frozen
½ cup chopped fresh parsley
2 teaspoons dried tarragon
2 cloves garlic, crushed
4 whole chicken breasts (about 1 pound each), halved
Salt
Freshly ground pepper

Combine butter, chives, parsley, tarragon, and garlic and set aside. Wash and dry chicken breasts, then salt and pepper them. Divide butter mixture into 8 equal parts. Stuff 1 part under the skin of each chicken breast, spreading it throughout the skin. Place chicken breasts skin-side down on aluminum foil or on a broiling pan and broil 13 to 15 minutes. Turn skin-side up and broil 13 to 15 minutes more, basting frequently with the pan drippings. Serve hot with the pan drippings poured over the chicken.

3.4 grams of carbohydrate in entire recipe; if serving 4, each serving contains 0.9 grams of carbohydrate.
2,404 calories in entire recipe; if serving 4, each serving contains 601 calories.

CHICKEN WITH CREAM AND HERBS

Makes 4 servings. The nutmeg in this recipe adds the high note.

3 whole chicken breasts (about 1 pound each), halved
Salt
Freshly ground pepper
1½ tablespoons butter

2 teaspoons oil
3 tablespoons minced shallots
6 tablespoons dry white wine or dry vermouth
6 tablespoons dry sherry
6 tablespoons chicken broth
6 tablespoons heavy cream
2 egg yolks
2 tablespoons minced parsley
2 tablespoons minced chives
Generous dash of freshly ground nutmeg

Wash and dry chicken breasts and sprinkle with salt and pepper. Heat butter and oil together in a large skillet. (The oil will keep the butter from burning.) Sauté the shallots lightly, then add chicken breasts, and brown until tender. Remove to a warm platter and pour off excess fat from the pan.

   Mix together the wine, sherry, and chicken broth. Deglaze the pan with this mixture, scraping up any browned bits. Cook the liquid for a few minutes until the alcohol smell evaporates. Beat the egg yolks with the cream and add to the pan, stirring constantly until heated (do not allow to boil). Add chives, parsley, and a dash of nutmeg to the sauce. To serve, spoon the sauce over the chicken breasts and serve hot.

7.0 grams of carbohydrate in entire recipe; if serving 4, each serving contains 1.8 grams of carbohydrate.

2,074 calories in entire recipe; if serving 4, each serving contains 519 calories.

SOY-GLAZED CHICKEN BREASTS

Serves 3

2 rounded tablespoons sugarless diet orange marmalade
Artificial sweetener equal to 2 tablespoons sugar
3 whole chicken breasts (about 1 pound each), halved
Salt

Pepper
Garlic powder
3 tablespoons soy sauce
⅓ cup water
1–2 tablespoons minced fresh ginger root

Combine orange marmalade and sweetener and set aside. Halve the chicken breasts, then wash and dry them. Sprinkle lightly with salt, pepper, and garlic powder. Arrange in broiling pan or on aluminum foil skin-side down.

Combine soy sauce, water, and ginger root, baste the chicken with this mixture, and broil 13 to 15 minutes. Turn chicken skin-side up, cover with remaining soy sauce mixture, and broil 13 to 15 minutes longer, basting frequently with pan drippings. When chicken is almost done, spread with the marmalade mixture, and broil 2 to 3 minutes longer. To serve, pour a little of the soy mixture from the pan on the chicken.

8.4 grams of carbohydrate in entire recipe; makes 3 servings, each serving containing 2.8 grams of carbohydrate.
450 calories in entire recipe; makes 3 servings, each serving containing 150 calories.

CURRIED CHICKEN BREASTS

Makes 4 servings

8 *suprêmes* (See NOTE)
1 teaspoon lemon juice
1 teaspoon salt
White pepper
4 tablespoons (½ stick) butter
½ cup chicken stock
½ cup dry white wine
½ cup heavy cream
¾–1 teaspoon curry powder

Preheat oven to 400° F. Rub the *suprêmes* with lemon juice, and sprinkle with salt and pepper. In 2 large ovenproof skillets or casseroles, heat the butter until foamy. Roll the *suprêmes* in the hot butter, putting 4 in each skillet. Cover each skillet with buttered waxed paper, cut to fit, and a regular cover. Place in preheated oven and cook 7 to 8 minutes or until chicken feels firm and slightly springy when tested with your finger. Remove to a hot serving platter leaving butter in the pans. Keep warm.

Add chicken broth and wine to the skillets, and boil over a high flame until the liquid becomes slightly syrupy. Add the cream and curry powder and boil for another minute or 2 until slightly thickened. Pour the sauce over the *suprêmes* and serve hot.

4.9 grams of carbohydrate in entire recipe; if serving 4, each serving contains 1.2 grams of carbohydrate.

2,148 calories in entire recipe; if serving 4, each serving contains 537 calories.

NOTE: To quote Julia Child, "Breast of chicken, when it is removed raw from one side of the bird in a skinless, boneless piece, is called a *'suprême.'* Each chicken possesses two of them."

CURRIED CHICKEN SALAD

Makes 6 servings. Curry powder makes an interesting and delicious variation for chicken salad.

3 cups cooked chicken, diced
2 cups diced celery
1 cup sugarless mayonnaise
2–3 teaspoons curry powder
Dash of garlic powder
Cantaloupe wedges

Combine diced chicken and diced celery. Mix in the mayonnaise. Add 2 or 3 teaspoons of curry powder, depending on the degree of spiciness you like, and a dash of garlic powder. Mix all ingredients thoroughly and serve scoops of the chicken salad on lettuce leaves. Cantaloupe wedges served on the side make a good taste contrast.

15.6 grams of carbohydrate in entire recipe; if serving 6, each serving contains 2.6 grams of carbohydrate.

2,492 calories in entire recipe; if serving 6, each serving contains 415 calories.

CHICKEN LIVER SAUTÉ

Makes 4 servings. Even people who don't like liver frequently like chicken livers.

2 slices bacon, cut into small pieces
1 small onion, chopped
1 tablespoon butter
1 pound chicken livers
½ cup sliced mushrooms
3 tablespoons Chablis or similar dry white wine
¼ teaspoon sage (a pinch more if desired)
Salt and freshly ground pepper to taste

Sauté the bacon and onion together. Add butter, chicken livers, and mushrooms and cook, stirring frequently, until the livers are browned but pink inside. Add the wine, sage, salt, and pepper and cook 2 minutes longer. Serve piping hot as an appetizer or light luncheon dish or use as a filling for a French omelet.

23.1 grams of carbohydrate in entire recipe; if serving 4, each serving contains 5.8 grams of carbohydrate.

851 calories in entire recipe; if serving 4, each serving contains 213 calories.

GLAZED ROCK CORNISH HENS

Makes 6 to 8 servings. The inspiration for these hens came from a Sunset cookbook and they make one of the most impressive meals you can serve.

4 frozen Rock Cornish game hens, thawed, each weighing about 1¾
    to 2 pounds
Salt
Freshly ground black pepper
8 tablespoons (1 stick) butter or margarine
4 tablespoons chopped chives, fresh or frozen
1 teaspoon dried rosemary, crushed
2 tablespoons lemon juice
¼ cup dietetic apricot jam
Artificial sweetener equal to 8 teaspoons sugar

Preheat oven to 350° F. Wash the hens thoroughly, then dry inside and outside with paper towels. Sprinkle the skin and cavities with salt and pepper.

Melt the butter, remove it from the heat, and add the chives and rosemary. Place about 1 tablespoon of the melted butter mixture inside each hen. Close the hens with small metal skewers or toothpicks. Tie the legs together with clean string. Add the lemon juice to the remaining butter mixture. Place hens in a roasting pan, breast side up. Baste them with the herb-flavored butter and roast them in a 350° F. oven for about 1 hour, turning the hens occasionally and basting with the herb-flavored butter. After 1 hour, raise the oven temperature to 575° F. to brown and crispen the skin.

Warm the apricot jam, remove it from the flame and add the artificial sweetener to it. When the hens are almost done, brush them evenly with the jam and continue roasting them until nicely glazed. Remove the string and serve hot.

6.7 grams of carbohydrate in entire recipe; if serving 8, each serving contains 0.8 grams of carbohydrate.

3,908 calories in entire recipe; if serving 8, each serving contains 489 calories.

PARTY CORNISH HENS

Makes 6 to 8 servings

Four 2-pound Rock Cornish hens
¼ cup Japanese soy sauce
¼ cup dry sherry
¼ cup peanut oil
1 small clove garlic, minced

Preheat the oven to 350° F. Wash and dry the hens thoroughly, then arrange them in a roasting pan. Mix together the soy sauce, sherry, oil, and garlic. Brush the hens with the soy sauce mixture. Use any remaining sauce to baste the hens as they cook. Roast 1 hour in preheated oven, then turn the heat up to 550° F. for 10 to 15 minutes more to brown the hens. Remove from the heat and serve immediately.

6.6 grams of carbohydrate in entire recipe; if serving 8, each serving contains 0.8 grams of carbohydrate.

3,687 calories in entire recipe; if serving 8, each serving contains 461 calories.

VII.
EGGS & EGG DISHES:
THANKS TO THE CHICKENS

Eggs & Egg Dishes:
Thanks to the Chickens

This chapter could almost have been called "Omelets Aplenty." Eggs are delicious by themselves when well prepared, but omelets are the most delicious of all. Give an omelet an interesting filling and it can be used for breakfast, lunch, or dinner.

CHEDDAR SCRAMBLED EGGS

Serves 1. Eggs and cheese are just meant for each other.

2 eggs
1 ounce very sharp white Cheddar cheese, grated
2 teaspoons butter

Break eggs into a bowl and beat thoroughly with a wire whisk. Add grated cheese to eggs. Melt butter in a Teflon-lined skillet and add egg mixture, stirring frequently to allow all uncooked egg to reach the bottom of the pan. Use a medium-low flame. As eggs set, cheese will begin to melt, streaking the eggs with melted cheese. Cook until you see there are no more separate pieces of cheese, then remove to a warm plate. Garnish with freshly chopped parsley and sprinkle generously with freshly ground black pepper. I like to keep some fresh, chopped parsley frozen in a plastic container in the freezer so I can just reach for it without having to chop it each time.

1.6 grams of carbohydrate in entire recipe; if serving 1, the serving contains 1.6 grams of carbohydrate.

369 calories in entire recipe; if serving 1, the serving contains the 369 calories.

EDAM SCRAMBLED EGGS

Serves 1. Try Edam Scrambled Eggs with slices of Nova Scotia smoked salmon on the side.

2 eggs
4 tablespoons grated Edam cheese (about 1½ ounces)
2 teaspoons butter

Break eggs into a bowl and beat thoroughly with a wire whisk. Add grated cheese to eggs. Melt butter in a Teflon-coated skillet, pour in egg mixture, and cook over lowest heat possible until the cheese has melted, stirring frequently. Once the cheese has melted, raise heat to medium and allow eggs to set, raising cooked parts with a spatula to allow uncooked parts to flow to the bottom to cook. When eggs are completely cooked to your taste, remove to a warm plate. Sprinkle with a generous quantity of freshly ground black pepper.

1.5 grams of carbohydrate in entire recipe; if serving 1, the serving contains the 1.5 grams of carbohydrate.

414 calories in entire recipe; if serving 1, the serving contains 414 calories.

CURRIED EGGS WITH LOBSTER

Makes 1 serving. Lobster, eggs, cream and curry—yummy! What a lunch!

¼ cup lobster meat, diced
2 teaspoons butter
Dash of paprika
¼ to ½ teaspoon curry powder, more or less depending upon the brand of curry powder used
⅛ teaspoon salt
2 eggs
4 teaspoons cream

Melt the butter in a heavy, Teflon-coated skillet. Add the diced lobster and sauté it for a minute just to heat it. Combine the paprika, curry powder, and salt and add it to the lobster meat. Beat the eggs with the cream only long enough to combine them, then add them to the lobster. Mix them in thoroughly, and continue cooking over low heat just until the eggs begin to set.

2.1 grams of carbohydrate in entire recipe; if serving 1, the serving contains the 2.1 grams of carbohydrate.
363 calories in entire recipe; if serving 1, the serving contains the 363 calories.

POACHED EGGS NÎMES

Makes 2 servings. Even people who don't like poached eggs like this recipe.

1 tablespoon melted butter
½ cup dry white wine
4 eggs
Salt

Pepper
Dash of cayenne pepper
2 tablespoons grated Roquefort cheese

Melt butter in a skillet, then add the wine. Slip in eggs, 1 at a time, taking care not to break yolks. Season with salt, pepper, and cayenne. Poach until egg whites are almost firm. Sprinkle with cheese and cook until cheese is melted.

2.5 grams of carbohydrate in entire recipe; if serving 2, each serving contains 1.3 grams of carbohydrate.
611 calories in entire recipe; if serving 2, each serving contains 306 calories.

Recipe for Poached Eggs Nîmes appeared in *The White House Chef Cookbook* by Rene Verdon.

Omelets Aplenty

GENERAL DIRECTIONS FOR OMELET MAKING

Have a separate pan you use only for omelets. This pan should not be washed once it is seasoned. If anything sticks to the pan, just rub it with a little coarse salt. Otherwise, merely wipe the pan out with a paper towel.

Have the eggs at room temperature. To bring the eggs to room temperature quickly, immerse them, before cracking, in a bowl of warm water. Dry the eggs and you are ready to make your omelet.

Beat the eggs with either cream or cold water only long enough to blend them. Do not overbeat or the omelet will be tough. An omelet should contain 2 or 3 eggs only. Do not attempt to use more eggs as it will be too hard to handle.

Heat the omelet pan over high heat until a few drops of water sizzle when sprinkled on it. Lower the flame to medium and put in the butter. Spread the butter around the pan with a fork until it covers the sides and bottom. Add the eggs and make about 8 to 10 circular turns with the fork to raise layers of fluffiness, at the same time shaking the pan back and forth with your hand. Work fast.

When all the liquid has set and the top of the omelet appears glossy, add the filling to the third of the omelet farthest from the handle. Change the position of your hand so that your palm is facing up when you hold the pan and begin rolling the omelet. Raise the handle and gently roll the omelet with the fork. Turn the omelet onto a warm plate by tilting the pan over completely. The entire process should take 1 to 1½ minutes. Serve the omelet immediately while warm.

CAVIAR OMELET

Makes 1 serving. The epitome of elegance in an omelet.

2 eggs
1 teaspoon heavy cream
1 tablespoon sour cream
1 teaspoon minced chives
1 tablespoon butter
2 teaspoons red or black caviar

Beat the eggs lightly with the heavy cream only until blended. Mix together the sour cream and chives and set aside. Make the omelet following general directions on page 155. Turn the omelet onto a warm plate. Top with a dollop of sour cream and chives and place the 2 teaspoons of caviar on top of the sour cream. Serve immediately while warm.

1.6 grams of carbohydrate in entire recipe.
337 calories in entire recipe.

DOUBLE CHEESE OMELET

Makes 1 serving

2 eggs
1 teaspoon heavy cream
1 teaspoon grated Parmesan cheese
2 teaspoons butter
1 tablespoon heavy cream
1 tablespoon grated Gruyère cheese

Break the eggs into a bowl and beat with the teaspoon of cream just until blended. Do not overbeat. Stir in the grated Parmesan cheese. Heat the butter in a Teflon-lined omelet pan and prepare as in General Directions for Omelet Making (page 155). Before folding over the omelet, pour the tablespoon of cream over eggs and sprinkle with grated Gruyère cheese, then turn over onto a plate.

2.0 grams of carbohydrate in entire recipe.
388 calories in entire recipe.

CHEESE AND HERB OMELET

Makes 1 serving

2 eggs
2 teaspoons heavy cream
2 tablespoons minced parsley
1 tablespoon minced chives
¼ cup grated Gruyère cheese
1 tablespoon butter

Beat eggs with cream only enough to blend them. Follow General Directions for Omelet Making (page 155), sprinkling the omelet with parsley, chives, and grated cheese in that order before turning.

2.5 grams of carbohydrate in entire recipe.
390 calories in entire recipe.

NOTE: L'Etoile was a French restaurant in New York that served a lovely buffet brunch on Saturdays and Sundays. When I couldn't decide whether I'd rather have *fines herbes* or cheese in my omelet, the chef suggested I have both. This is the result of his suggestion.

MY FAVORITE OMELET

Makes 1 serving. This title speaks for itself.

2 slices Canadian bacon
2 eggs
1 teaspoon heavy cream
1 ounce Gruyère cheese (not the processed version)
1 teaspoon chopped chives, fresh, frozen, or freeze-dried
1 tablespoon butter

Panbroil the Canadian bacon, then cut it in cubes. Break the eggs into a bowl and beat lightly with the cream. Cut the cheese in tiny cubes and add it, Canadian bacon, and chives to the eggs. Mix thoroughly. Heat the butter in a well-seasoned omelet pan or in a Teflon-lined omelet pan and prepare using General Directions for Omelet Making (page 155).

1.7 grams of carbohydrate in entire recipe.
509 calories in entire recipe.

FINES HERBES OMELET

Makes 1 serving. The herb butter topping makes all the difference.

1 tablespoon butter
1 teaspoon fresh chives, minced
1 teaspoon fresh tarragon, minced
1 teaspoon fresh parsley, minced
2 extra-large eggs
1 teaspoon heavy cream or cold water
1 teaspoon fresh chives, minced
1 teaspoon fresh tarragon, minced
1 teaspoon fresh parsley, minced
2 teaspoons butter

To make an herb butter, mix together 1 teaspoon each of fresh chives, fresh tarragon and fresh parsley. Melt the butter over a low flame and add the seasonings.

Meanwhile beat the eggs with the cream or water only enough to blend them. Add the remaining chives, tarragon and parsley to the eggs. Make the omelet following General Directions for Omelet Making (page 155). Turn the omelet onto a warm plate and pour the herb butter over it. Serve immediately while warm.

1.1 grams of carbohydrate in entire recipe.
376 calories in entire recipe.

FINES HERBES SOUFFLÉ OMELET

Makes 1 serving. A puffy version of a Fines Herbes Omelet.

2 extra-large eggs, separated
¼ teaspoon cream of tartar
1 tablespoon heavy cream
2 tablespoons chopped chives, fresh, frozen or freeze-dried

2 tablespoons chopped fresh parsley
¼ teaspoon dried tarragon
1 tablespoon butter

Beat egg whites until foamy, add cream of tartar and continue beating until stiff but not dry. Beat the egg yolks lightly with the cream. Add the chives, parsley, and tarragon to the egg yolks. Very gently, fold the beaten egg whites into the egg yolk mixture, being careful not to break down the egg whites. Melt one tablespoon butter in an 8-inch Teflon-lined omelet pan or well-seasoned iron omelet pan. Pour in the eggs. Fry until golden brown on the bottom (yes, you may peek) and set on top. Slide one half of the omelet onto a warm plate, then fold in half. Serve immediately.

1.5 grams of carbohydrate in entire recipe.
345 calories in entire recipe.

GREEK OMELET

Makes 1 serving. The Feta cheese gives this omelet a nice Greek touch.

2 eggs
1 teaspoon heavy cream
1 tablespoon minced parsley
1 teaspoon minced chives
¼ cup crumbled Greek Feta cheese
1 tablespoon butter

Beat the eggs with the cream only long enough to blend them. Make the omelet following General Directions for Omelet Making (page 155). Sprinkle the omelet with the herbs, then with the Feta cheese before turning.

1.7 grams of carbohydrate in entire recipe.
408 calories in entire recipe.

HAM OMELET

Makes 1 serving. This omelet was my favorite breakfast at The Gray Gull Inn in Nantucket, Mass.

2 eggs
1 teaspoon heavy cream
3 tablespoons chopped ham
1 tablespoon unsalted butter

Beat eggs with cream only enough to blend them. Mix in the chopped ham. Follow General Directions for Omelet Making (page 155).

1.4 grams of carbohydrate in entire recipe.
351 calories in entire recipe.

HAM AND CHEESE OMELET

Makes 1 serving

1 recipe Ham Omelet
2 tablespoons grated Gruyère cheese

Follow instructions for Ham Omelet, sprinkling the omelet with the grated cheese before turning it.

1.7 grams of carbohydrate in entire recipe.
401 calories in entire recipe.

HAM-MUSHROOM OMELET

Makes 1 serving

½ tablespoon butter
2 ounces firm white mushrooms—this is about 3 small mushrooms or
    2 large ones
¼ cup diced ham
1 tablespoon sour cream
⅛ teaspoon dried tarragon
¼ teaspoon chives, fresh, frozen, or freeze-dried
Dash salt and pepper
2 eggs, at room temperature
1 teaspoon heavy cream
1 tablespoon butter

Melt ½ teaspoon butter in a heavy skillet, add the mushrooms, and
sauté them for about two minutes. Add the ham and sauté for 2 to 3
minutes more. The mushrooms should remain rather firm. Lower the
flame, mix in the sour cream, tarragon, chives, salt and pepper. Heat
only long enough to warm the sour cream.

Beat the eggs with a teaspoon of heavy cream only enough to
blend the eggs. Make omelet following General Directions for
Omelet Making (page 155). Before turning, spread the mushroom-
ham mixture over the eggs. Turn out onto a warm plate and serve
immediately.

4.3 grams of carbohydrate in entire recipe.
496 calories in entire recipe.

ITALIAN CHEESE OMELET

Makes 1 serving. A rich, creamy omelet.

2 eggs
2 teaspoons water
1 tablespoon butter

2 ounces ricotta—a scant ¼ cup
1 ounce finely chopped or grated mixed Italian cheeses

Have all ingredients at room temperature. Beat the eggs with the water only long enough to combine them. Follow General Directions for Omelet Making (page 155) filling the omelet with the ricotta and then with the mixed cheeses before turning it.

4.2 grams of carbohydrate in entire recipe.
388 calories in entire recipe.

NOTE: You may include any Italian cheeses you have on hand but try to include a little mozzarella and grated Parmesan. I combine any or all of the following—mozzarella, Parmesan, Bel Paese, Fontina, Teleggio, and Provolone.

MUSHROOM, HERBS AND CHEESE OMELET

Makes 1 serving. Madame Romaine de Lyon is a restaurant in New York that serves authentic French omelets with hundreds of different flavorings. This is one of the ones I have eaten there.

3 medium sized mushrooms
1 tablespoon butter
1 tablespoon chopped chives, fresh or frozen
2 eggs
2 teaspoons heavy cream
½ cup grated Swiss Emmenthal cheese
1 tablespoon butter

Sauté the mushrooms in 1 tablespoon butter. Remove from heat, add the chives and set aside. Beat the eggs with the cream only long enough to blend them. Make the omelet following General Directions for Omelet Making (page 155), spreading the eggs with the mushrooms and then the cheese before turning it.

6.0 grams of carbohydrate in entire recipe.
654 calories in entire recipe.

MUSHROOM SOUFFLÉ OMELET

Makes 1 serving

¼ pound firm white mushrooms, thinly sliced
1 tablespoon butter
½ teaspoon lemon juice
¼ teaspoon salt
Generous dash of freshly ground black pepper
2 extra-large eggs, at room temperature, separated
¼ teaspoon cream of tartar
1 tablespoon heavy cream
Another dash of freshly ground black pepper
1 tablespoon butter

Sauté the mushrooms in 1 tablespoon butter with the lemon juice, salt, and pepper.

Beat egg whites until foamy, add cream of tartar, and continue beating until stiff but not dry. Beat egg yolks lightly with the heavy cream and a little freshly ground pepper. Very gently fold the beaten whites into the yolk mixture, being careful not to break down the whites.

Melt 1 tablespoon of butter in an 8-inch Teflon-lined pan or well-seasoned omelet pan. Pour in the eggs.

Fry until golden brown on the bottom (yes, you may peek) and set on top. Spread with the sautéed mushrooms, reserving about 1 tablespoon of mushrooms as a garnish. Slide half of the omelet onto the center of a warm plate, then fold the remaining half over the top. Garnish with the reserved mushrooms. Serve immediately.

6.7 grams of carbohydrate in entire recipe.
478 calories in entire recipe.

CHEESE, TOMATO, AND HERB OMELET

Makes 1 serving. Serve this omelet unfolded like an Italian *frittata*.

2 teaspoons butter
½ medium-sized tomato, sliced thinly
2 eggs
1 teaspoon heavy cream
2 teaspoons water
Salt
Freshly ground black pepper
1 teaspoon chives, minced
1 teaspoon parsley, minced
2 ounces Gruyère cheese, grated

Place the butter in a 6- to 7-inch Teflon-coated skillet and heat to sizzling. Arrange the tomato slices in the butter in a single layer. Beat the eggs with the cream, water, salt and pepper only long enough to combine them and add them to the pan, raising the tomato slices to allow the eggs to run to the bottom of the pan. Sprinkle the top with the chives and parsley, then with the grated Gruyère cheese. Continue to cook the eggs over a low flame only long enough for the cheese to melt.

6.5 grams of carbohydrate in entire recipe.
514 calories in entire recipe.

Soufflés

CHEESE SOUFFLÉ

Makes 4 servings. The first soufflé I ever made was a miserable failure, but I only failed once, so don't be discouraged! You'll soon be making high, light, and puffy ones.

2 tablespoons butter
2 tablespoons full-fat soy flour
½ cup heavy cream
½ cup cold water
½ teaspoon salt
Dash of white pepper
¾ cup (about 3 ounces) grated, sharp Cheddar cheese
Dash of nutmeg
Dash of cayenne pepper
2 egg yolks
6 whole eggs, at room temperature, separated
¾ teaspoon cream of tartar

Preheat oven to 400° F. Butter a 6-cup soufflé dish. Make a waxed paper or foil collar for it, and set it aside.

Melt butter in a heavy saucepan over low heat. With a wire whisk, stir in the soy flour. Cook for a few minutes until thoroughly blended. Combine cream and water and add slowly to the butter-flour mixture, stirring constantly with the whisk. Add the salt and pepper and heat to scalding. Then add the cheese, nutmeg, and cayenne. When the cheese has melted, beat in the 2 egg yolks, 1 at a time. Heat a few more minutes, but do not allow mixture to boil. Remove from the heat. Separate the remaining 6 eggs and beat in the yolks, 1 at a time. Beat egg whites until foamy, add cream of tartar, and continue beating until stiff but not dry. Fold about a fourth of the egg whites into the cheese sauce thoroughly, then very gently fold in the remainder, being careful not to break the whites down. Turn soufflé batter into the prepared dish and bake 25 to 30 minutes. Remove from the oven and serve immediately.

13.1 grams of carbohydrate in entire recipe; if serving 4, each serving contains 3.3 grams of carbohydrate.

1,712 calories in entire recipe; if serving 4, each serving contains 428 calories.

GOURMET SOUFFLÉ

Makes 4 to 5 servings. Swiss Gruyère and Parmesan are my favorite combination of cheeses for a soufflé.

Follow directions for Cheese Soufflé (page 166), adding *1 cup of grated Gruyère cheese* (approximately ¼ pound), and *¼ cup grated Parmesan cheese* in place of the Cheddar cheese. Bake the soufflé at 425° F. for 25 minutes.

14.8 grams of carbohydrate in entire recipe; if serving 4, each serving contains 3.7 grams of carbohydrate.

1,979 calories in entire recipe; if serving 4, each serving contains 495 calories.

MÜNSTER-CARAWAY SOUFFLÉ

Makes 4 servings

2 tablespoons butter
2 tablespoons full-fat soy flour
½ cup heavy cream
½ cup cold water
Dash of cayenne pepper
½ teaspoon salt, or to taste
Dash of white pepper
1 cup diced Münster cheese (¼ pound)
½ teaspoon caraway seeds
2 egg yolks
4 whole eggs
1 extra egg white
½ teaspoon cream of tartar

Follow directions for Cheese Soufflé (page 166) substituting Münster cheese for Cheddar cheese. Add the caraway seeds to the cheese sauce. Bake in a 1½-quart soufflé dish at 375° F. for 30 to 35 minutes.

11.5 grams of carbohydrate in entire recipe; if serving 4, each serving contains 2.9 grams of carbohydrate.

1,594 calories in entire recipe; if serving 4, each serving contains 399 calories.

VIII.
VEGETABLES & SALADS:
GIFTS FROM THE EARTH

Vegetables & Salads:
Gifts from the Earth

I could have given many more recipes for fancy ways to prepare vegetables; however, I feel that it's a crime to doctor them up too much. The trick to making vegetables delicious is to avoid overcooking them. Do as the Chinese do and use color as a guide to judging when the vegetables are cooked. Green vegetables should remain bright green; when they become dull, it means they are overcooked. Use a steamer, pressure cooker, or heavy saucepan placed over high heat with very little water, and above all, keep the vegetables crisp. Picture crisp asparagus, broccoli, green beans, zucchini or cauliflower with melted butter—heaven on earth!

BAKED ARTICHOKE HEARTS

Makes 3 servings

1 box frozen artichoke hearts
Salt
½ tablespoon olive oil
2 tablespoons butter, melted
¼ cup grated Parmesan cheese

Preheat oven to 350° F. Cook artichokes in salted water for 5 minutes. Mix together the oil and melted butter. Drain artichoke hearts

170

thoroughly and place in a shallow 7-inch baking dish. Pour the oil-butter mixture over them and mix in thoroughly. Bake for 5 minutes at 350° F., then raise the oven temperature to 450° F., top artichokes with Parmesan cheese, and bake for 10 to 12 minutes.

14.3 grams of carbohydrate in entire recipe; if serving 3, each serving contains 4.8 grams of carbohydrate.
439 calories in entire recipe; if serving 3, each serving contains 146 calories.

GREEN BEANS AMANDINE

Makes 5 servings. A delicate, delicious method for preparing green beans.

1 pound very tiny green beans
2 quarts water
1 tablespoon salt
2 tablespoons butter
3 tablespoons slivered almonds, toasted
Additional salt to taste
Freshly ground black pepper to taste

Trim the ends from the beans. Bring water to a boil, add salt and beans, then return to boil and cook beans, uncovered, for 8 to 10 minutes. Beans should be crisp-tender. Test 1 by eating it. Set the color by running beans under cold water. Dry with paper towels. Melt butter in a skillet, add the beans, and toss in the butter. Mix in the toasted almonds. Serve hot.

34.0 grams of carbohydrate in entire recipe; if serving 5, each serving contains 6.8 grams of carbohydrate.
502 calories in entire recipe; if serving 5, each serving contains 100 calories.

MY MOTHER'S STUFFED CABBAGE

Makes 12 cabbage bundles

12 large cabbage leaves
1 pound very lean ground beef
1 tablespoon minced onion
¼ teaspoon salt, or to taste
Generous sprinkling of freshly ground black pepper
Artificial sweetener equal to ⅛ teaspoon sugar
⅔ cup tomato sauce
¼ teaspoon salt
Dash of freshly ground black pepper
2 tablespoons fresh lemon juice
2 cups cold water
Artificial sweetener equal to 3 tablespoons sugar
Brown sugar artificial sweetener equal to 1 tablespoon brown sugar

Buy a large, very loose head of cabbage as the leaves will be easier to separate. Soften cabbage leaves in boiling water for 5 minutes, then remove, and drain thoroughly.

Mix together the ground beef, minced onion, ¼ teaspoon of salt, black pepper, and artificial sweetener equal to ⅛ teaspoon sugar. Divide the meat into 12 equal parts. Place 1 part on 1 cabbage leaf, tuck in the sides, and carefully roll it up. Repeat this procedure until all 12 leaves are rolled. Carefully tie each cabbage bundle with heavy-weight, white sewing thread (6 or 8 cord), to hold together during cooking.

In a heavy saucepan, combine the tomato sauce, ¼ teaspoon salt, dash of pepper, lemon juice, cold water, and both artificial sweeteners. Bring this mixture to a boil and carefully place cabbage bundles in it. Cover the pot, lower the flame, and simmer 1 hour. Taste sauce and correct seasoning. The sauce should be both sweet and sour. Serve hot with sauce spooned over the bundles. Stuffed cabbage can be served either as an appetizer or as a main course.

35.0 grams of carbohydrate in entire recipe; makes 12 cabbage bundles, each one containing 2.9 grams of carbohydrate.

970 calories in entire recipe; makes 12 cabbage bundles, each one containing 81 calories.

These figures are based upon the cabbage being served with the sauce.

NOTE: One tablespoon of brown sugar equals 1 tablespoon of Brown Sugar Twin (page 13).

CAULIFLOWER WITH CHEESE

Makes 6 servings

1 large cauliflower (about 3 pounds before trimming)
Salt
2 tablespoons whipped butter
¼ pound grated sharp white Cheddar cheese
Freshly ground black pepper

Preheat oven to 400° F. Cook the cauliflower whole in salted water to cover 20 to 25 minutes until crisp-tender. Drain thoroughly. Place the cauliflower in a round snugly fitting baking dish. A soufflé dish is nice for this. Dot the cauliflower with whipped butter and grated cheese. Bake until the cheese melts and browns slightly. Serve immediately.

30.5 grams of carbohydrate in entire recipe; if serving 6, each serving contains 5.1 grams of carbohydrate.

1,014 calories in entire recipe; if serving 6, each serving contains 169 calories.

FRIED CAULIFLOWER

Makes 8 servings. A dressed up version of cauliflower.

1 large cauliflower (3 pounds before trimming), cooked crisp-tender
2 tablespoons Seasoned Soy Flour (page 22)
2 extra-large eggs
2 tablespoons oil
2 teaspoons butter

Separate the cooked cauliflower into flowerets. Dredge flowerets lightly in the Seasoned Soy Flour. Beat the eggs, then dip the flowerets into the eggs. Heat the oil and butter together in a heavy skillet, add the cauliflower, and fry until golden brown on all sides. Serve immediately while hot.

34.5 grams of carbohydrate in entire recipe; if serving 8, each serving contains 4.3 grams of carbohydrate.
694 calories in entire recipe; if serving 8, each serving contains 87 calories.

BRAISED SLICED CELERY

Makes 3 servings

3 tablespoons butter
1 pound celery stalks sliced at a diagonal (about 5 cups)
3 tablespoons chicken broth
½ teaspoon salt
Generous dash of freshly ground black pepper

Melt butter in a heavy skillet over medium heat. Add sliced celery and mix thoroughly for 2 to 3 minutes until celery is completely coated with butter. Add chicken broth, salt, and pepper, cover the pan, and cook for 10 to 12 minutes until celery is crisp-tender and the pan juices have thickened. Serve hot.

13.6 grams of carbohydrate in entire recipe; if serving 3, each serving contains 4.5 grams of carbohydrate.

366 calories in entire recipe; if serving 3, each serving contains 122 calories.

CELERY GRUYÈRE

Makes 3 servings. Cooked celery blends well with cheese.

Place 1 recipe Braised Sliced Celery (page 174) in a baking dish. Pour the pan juices over the celery. Sprinkle with ¼ cup grated Swiss gruyère cheese and place under the broiler until the cheese melts and browns.

14.1 grams of carbohydrate in entire recipe; if serving 3, each serving contains 4.7 grams of carbohydrate.

467 calories in entire recipe; if serving 3, each serving contains 156 calories.

MY MOTHER'S STUFFED EGGPLANT ROLL

Makes 12 rolls. This is a Mid-East specialty, a bit complicated to make, but definitely worth the trouble.

One 3-pound elongated eggplant
Salt
3 pounds very lean ground beef
3 tablespoons minced onion
1 teaspoon salt
Freshly ground black pepper
Artificial sweetener equal to ⅜ teaspoon sugar
6 extra-large eggs
5 tablespoons Seasoned Soy Flour (page 22)
4 tablespoons oil

Sauce:

2 cups tomato sauce
¼ cup lemon juice
Artificial sweetener equal to ¼ cup sugar
Brown sugar artificial sweetener equal to 1 tablespoon brown sugar

Peel the eggplant, then slice it lengthwise into ¼-inch slices making sure to remove the seeds. Sprinkle each slice lightly on both sides with salt and place in a deep bowl. The salt will soften the eggplant and make it give off its water. Allow to sit at least 1 hour. Meanwhile, mix together stuffing ingredients—beef, onion, salt, pepper, artificial sweetener and 3 eggs—and set aside.

Squeeze any remaining water from the eggplant by pressing the slices with paper towels. Reserve the 12 broadest center slices of eggplant. Cut up the remaining eggplant slices and place them over the center parts of the eggplant. Divide the meat mixture into 12 equal parts and place 1 part on each slice of eggplant. Roll up slices and tie each with 6 or 8 cord white thread.

Beat remaining 3 eggs. Dredge each eggplant roll in Seasoned Soy Flour (page 22), then dip in beaten egg. Heat 2 tablespoons of the oil in each of 2 large skillets and fry rolls until golden brown on all sides.

In a shallow 3½-quart casserole, heat together the tomato sauce, lemon juice, and remaining artificial sweeteners. Add eggplant rolls to the sauce, cover pan, lower flame to simmer, and cook 1 hour. To serve, spoon sauce over the eggplant rolls and serve hot.

113.9 grams of carbohydrate in entire recipe; makes 12 eggplant rolls, each containing 9.5 grams of carbohydrate.

4,621 calories in entire recipe; makes 12 eggplant rolls, each containing 385 calories.

BROILED EGGPLANT SLICES

Makes 4 servings. Try this recipe on an outdoor grill if you have a backyard or a terrace.

One 1-pound eggplant
6 tablespoons olive oil
2 tablespoons mild wine vinegar
1 clove garlic, crushed
Generous sprinkling of freshly ground black pepper
Salt

Slice the eggplant into ½-inch slices. Combine olive oil, vinegar, garlic and pepper. Place eggplant slices on a sheet of aluminum foil or on a broiling pan, brush with half the oil and vinegar mixture, and broil until golden brown. Turn the slices, brush with the remaining oil and vinegar, and broil until the other side is golden brown. Remove from the heat, sprinkle with salt, and serve hot.

22.6 grams of carbohydrate in entire recipe; if serving 4, each serving contains 5.7 grams of carbohydrate.
787 calories in entire recipe; if serving 4, each serving contains 197 calories.

BRAISED ENDIVE

Makes 6 servings. Endive is as delicious served hot as a vegetable as it is when served cold in a salad.

2 pounds endive
4 tablespoons (½ stick) butter
½ cup chicken stock

Wash endive, then dry in paper towels. Melt the butter in a large, heavy skillet. Add endive to the pan and roll in the melted butter until all pieces are completely coated. Add chicken stock, cover pan, and cook over low heat 40 to 45 minutes or until liquid has evaporated and endive is golden brown. Turn the endive to brown all sides. Serve hot.

26.5 grams of carbohydrate in entire recipe; if serving 6, each serving contains 4.4 grams of carbohydrate.
548 calories in entire recipe; if serving 6, each serving contains 91 calories.

SAUTÉED ESCAROLE

Makes 8 servings

2 pounds escarole
2 tablespoons olive oil
2 cloves garlic, minced
Salt
Freshly ground pepper
½ teaspoon oregano

Wash escarole in deep water in a clean sink. Repeat 2 or 3 times more. Dry with paper towels or in a salad spinner. Heat a Teflon-lined pan and add the oil and garlic to the pan. Add the escarole and sauté until tender or about 10 minutes. Mix in the oregano, salt and pepper to taste and cook for another 1 or 2 minutes. Serve hot.

33.6 grams of carbohydrate in entire recipe; if serving 8, each serving contains 4.2 grams of carbohydrate.
392 calories in entire recipe; if serving 8, each serving contains 49 calories.

MOCK PASTA

Makes 3 servings

1½ quarts water
2 teaspoons salt
1½ teaspoons oregano

1 teaspoon basil
¼ teaspoon onion powder
2 dashes garlic powder
¼ teaspoon freshly ground pepper
1 can Chinese bean sprouts
2–3 tablespoons butter
1–1½ cloves fresh garlic, crushed
¼ cup chopped fresh parsley
¼ cup grated Parmesan cheese
Salt
Freshly ground pepper
Chopped fresh basil leaves (optional)

Combine first 7 ingredients and bring to a boil. Add bean sprouts and return to a boil. Lower flame and simmer 20 minutes. Drain in a colander. Return bean sprouts to the pan and dry for 1 minute over high heat. Over high flame, toss with butter. Add garlic and remove from heat. Add parsley, fresh basil, and cheese and toss. Season with salt and freshly ground pepper to taste. Serve with additional grated Parmesan cheese.

12.2 grams of carbohydrate in entire recipe; if serving 3, each serving contains 4.1 grams of carbohydrate.
400 calories in entire recipe; if serving 3, each serving contains 133 calories.

CREAMED MUSHROOMS WITH CHEESE

Makes 4 servings. Try serving these mushrooms with a simple grilled steak and a tossed green salad.

2 tablespoons butter
1 tablespoon olive oil
1 pound firm, white fresh mushrooms, thinly sliced
2 tablespoons dry sherry
¼ cup sour cream
2 tablespoons freshly grated Parmesan cheese

Salt
Freshly ground black pepper to taste
Additional Parmesan cheese, if desired

Melt butter in a skillet. Add oil. (This helps prevent butter from burning.) Add sliced mushrooms and sauté 2 minutes. Add sherry and cook 1 minute more. Mix together sour cream, grated cheese, salt, and pepper and add to mushrooms. Cook over a low flame until sour cream has warmed thoroughly (do not boil). Add additional grated cheese, if desired. Serve while warm.

22.0 grams of carbohydrate in entire recipe; if serving 4, each serving contains 5.5 grams of carbohydrate.
603 calories in entire recipe; if serving 4, each serving contains 151 calories.

MY MOTHER'S STUFFED GREEN PEPPERS

Makes 8 large peppers

8 large green peppers

Stuffing:

3 pounds very lean ground beef
3 tablespoons minced onion
¾ teaspoon salt, or to taste
Generous sprinkling of freshly ground black pepper
Artificial sweetener equal to ⅜ teaspoon of sugar

Sauce:

1⅓ cups tomato sauce
¾ teaspoon salt
Generous sprinkling of freshly ground black pepper
¼ cup fresh lemon juice

2 cups cold water
Artificial sweetener equal to ¼ cup sugar
Brown sugar artificial sweetener equal to 2 tablespoons brown sugar

Cut a ½-inch piece across stem end of peppers and carefully remove all fibers and seeds. Wash and dry the peppers and set aside.

Mix together the ground beef, minced onion, salt, freshly ground black pepper, and artificial sweetener equal to ⅜ teaspoon sugar. Divide meat into 8 equal parts and stuff pepper cavities with it, pressing the meat down to the very bottom.

In a heavy saucepan, combine tomato sauce, ¾ teaspoon salt, freshly ground black pepper, lemon juice, cold water, and remaining artificial sweeteners. Bring this mixture to a boil, then place the stuffed peppers in it. Cover pot, lower flame and simmer 1 hour. Taste the sauce and correct seasoning.

Remove the stuffed peppers to a warm platter. Raise flame under the sauce, and boil to reduce and thicken. Spoon thickened sauce over the stuffed peppers and serve hot. You may serve the peppers whole or cut them in half lengthwise.

68.8 grams of carbohydrate in entire recipe; makes 8 peppers, each pepper containing 8.6 grams of carbohydrate.

2,724 calories in entire recipe; makes 8 peppers, each pepper containing 341 calories.

NOTE: These figures are based upon the peppers being served with the sauce. Stuffed peppers can be served either as an appetizer or as a main course, depending upon the size of the portions. One whole pepper makes a full main course.

CREAMED SPINACH

Makes 4 servings. Guaranteed to make people who hate spinach learn to love it.

2 packages frozen chopped spinach
3 tablespoons cold water
1 teaspoon salt

½ cup heavy cream
2 egg yolks
Generous dash of freshly ground nutmeg
Generous dash of freshly ground black pepper
Additional salt, if necessary

Cook the spinach with the water, covered, over high heat for approximately 4 minutes or until just defrosted. (Do not follow the directions on the package.) If there is any liquid left in pan, remove the cover and continue cooking 1 or 2 minutes more until liquid evaporates. Mix together the cream and egg yolks and add to spinach. Cook over low heat, stirring constantly, until spinach combines well with the cream mixture and thickens (do not boil). Season to taste with the nutmeg, pepper, and more salt if necessary.

20.8 grams of carbohydrate in entire recipe; if serving 4, each serving contains 5.2 grams of carbohydrate.
478 calories in entire recipe; if serving 4, each serving contains 120 calories.

SAUTÉED SPINACH

Makes 6 servings. The Italian method for preparing spinach.

2 pounds fresh spinach
2 tablespoons olive oil
2 cloves of garlic, minced
½ teaspoon salt
Generous amount of freshly ground black pepper

Follow directions for Sautéed Escarole (page 178), cutting the cooking time down to 5 to 6 minutes.

28.8 grams of carbohydrate in entire recipe; if serving 6, each serving contains 4.8 grams of carbohydrate.
402 calories in entire recipe; if serving 6, each serving contains 67 calories.

GRILLED TOMATOES WITH CHEESE

Serves 4. The inspiration for this recipe came from Elizabeth David, England's gift to the world of food.

½ pound Swiss Gruyère cheese
3 tablespoons dry white wine or vermouth
Generous dash freshly ground black pepper
Dash of cayenne
Dash of Dijon-style mustard
1 small clove garlic, put through a press
4 medium-sized tomatoes
Salt

Preheat oven to 350° F. Cube the cheese and place it in a heavy saucepan over very low heat. Mix in the wine, black pepper, cayenne, mustard and garlic. Heat until cheese melts and all ingredients are well blended, stirring frequently.

While the cheese is melting, cut off the tops from 4 medium-sized tomatoes. Scoop out the pulp and seeds. Sprinkle the tomato shells with salt, turn them upside down and allow them to drain. Fill each tomato shell with about 3 tablespoons of the melted cheese mixture. Place the tomatoes in individual ramekins if possible as it is difficult to pick them up later. Bake for 10 minutes, then remove them to the broiler and broil for a few minutes until the cheese mixture browns lightly. Serve immediately while hot.

20.8 grams of carbohydrate in entire recipe; makes 4 tomatoes, each containing 5.2 grams of carbohydrate.
883 calories in entire recipe; makes 4 tomatoes, each containing 221 calories.

MY MOTHER'S STUFFED ZUCCHINI

Makes 16 pieces. My mother spent four years in the Middle East before she was married. This is one of the specialties she learned to make while she was there. It's my favorite of all her stuffed vegetable recipes!

Four 1-pound zucchini (each 9–10 inches long)

Stuffing:

1 pound very lean ground beef
¼ teaspoon salt
Generous dash of freshly ground black pepper
1 tablespoon minced onion
Artificial sweetener equal to ⅛ teaspoon sugar

Sauce:

⅔ cup tomato sauce
¼ teaspoon salt, or to taste
Dash of freshly ground black pepper
2 tablespoons fresh lemon juice
1 cup cold water
Artificial sweetener equal to 3 tablespoons sugar
Brown sugar artificial sweetener equal to 1 tablespoon brown sugar

Trim the ends from the zucchini, then wash and dry. Do not peel. Cut each zucchini in two 4½- to 5-inch pieces. Scoop out each piece with an apple corer, discarding seeds and reserving flesh. Shells should be ¼ inch thick at sides and bottom.

For stuffing, mix together the ground beef, salt, black pepper, minced onion, and artificial sweetener equal to ⅛ teaspoon of sugar. Divide the meat into 8 equal parts and stuff zucchini cavities with it, pressing the meat down to the very bottom.

Make sauce in a heavy saucepan, combining tomato sauce, ¼ teaspoon salt, pepper, lemon juice, cold water, and artificial sweeteners. Bring this mixture to a boil, add reserved zucchini flesh, then lay the stuffed zucchini on top. Cover pot, lower flame and simmer 1 hour.

Taste the sauce (which may need salt) and correct seasoning. Remove stuffed zucchini to a warm platter and cut each one in half crosswise, to make 16 pieces. Raise flame under the sauce, and boil to reduce and thicken. Spoon thickened sauce over the stuffed zucchini and serve hot. The zucchini scoopings will have become part of the sauce.

72.7 grams of carbohydrate in entire recipe; makes 16 pieces, each piece containing 4.5 grams of carbohydrate.
1,145 calories in entire recipe; makes 16 pieces, each piece containing 72 calories.

NOTE: These figures are based upon the zucchini being served with the sauce. Stuffed zucchini can be served either as an appetizer or as a main course, depending upon the size of the portions.

ZUCCHINI WITH CHEESE

Makes 4 servings

1½ pounds 5–6-inch zucchini
Salt
1 tablespoon butter
3 tablespoons grated Parmesan cheese
Generous dash of freshly ground black pepper

Trim the ends from the zucchini, but do not peel. Cook whole in salted water to cover, 6 to 8 minutes, then drain. Slice zucchini into 1 inch rounds. Melt butter in a skillet, add zucchini, and toss lightly. Remove to a warm serving dish and stir in Parmesan cheese. Sprinkle with the freshly ground black pepper. Serve hot.

24.0 grams of carbohydrate in entire recipe; if serving 4, each serving contains 6.0 grams of carbohydrate.
290 calories in entire recipe; if serving 4, each serving contains 73 calories.

SALADE NIÇOISE

Makes 4 servings. My version of a delicious French main-dish salad. This salad was the hit of our beach house when served with Beach House Mustard Dressing (page 228).

10 large leaves romaine lettuce
Three 6½-ounce cans tuna fish, flaked
12 anchovy fillets, halved
12 black olives
½ cup cooked green beans
3 hard-cooked eggs, quartered
2 small tomatoes, quartered
8 marinated artichoke hearts

Arrange the lettuce leaves on a large platter. Mix together all remaining ingredients and arrange on the lettuce. Serve with Vinaigrette Dressing (page 227) or Beach House Mustard Dressing.

24.3 grams of carbohydrate in entire recipe; if serving 4, each serving contains 6.1 grams of carbohydrate.
1,407 calories in entire recipe; if serving 4, each serving contains 352 calories.

NOTE: This recipe can also be used in smaller portions as an appetizer as is frequently done in France.

BACON, SPINACH, AND MUSHROOM SALAD

Makes 8 servings. Try this as a main dish luncheon salad.

1 pound bacon
1 pound fresh spinach
1 pound small, firm, white mushrooms

¾ cup olive oil
¼ cup mild wine vinegar
2 tablespoons chopped fresh parsley
½ teaspoon Dijon-style mustard
½ teaspoon salt
Generous sprinkling of freshly ground black pepper

Broil bacon until crisp and drain on paper towels. Trim heavy stems from the spinach and wash thoroughly. Dry thoroughly in paper towels or in a salad spinner. Wipe mushrooms with a damp cloth or paper towel and slice. Mix spinach leaves and mushrooms together and crumble broiled bacon over all. Place the oil, vinegar, parsley, mustard, salt, and pepper in a blender and blend a few seconds at high speed. Toss the salad with this dressing.

41.2 grams of carbohydrate in entire recipe; if serving 8, each serving contains 5.2 grams of carbohydrate.
4,661 calories in entire recipe; if serving 8, each serving contains 583 calories.

CHEF'S SALAD

Makes 2 servings. A perennial favorite for lunch or dinner.

¼ pound imported Swiss Emmenthal cheese
¼ pound ham
¼ pound cooked white meat of chicken
6–8 lettuce leaves
2 hard-cooked eggs, halved
4 green pepper rings
16 thin slices cucumber
1 small tomato cut into wedges
2 scallions

Slice the cheese, ham, and chicken into Julienne strips about 2 to 3 inches long. Arrange lettuce on 2 plates, making a bed for the remaining ingredients. Divide all the ingredients in half. Arrange little piles of cheese, ham, and chicken on each plate, then decorate with the eggs and vegetables. Each plate should contain some of each of the ingredients. Serve with Vinaigrette dressing (page 227), Roquefort dressing (page 229), or mayonnaise.

24.3 grams of carbohydrate in entire recipe; if serving 2, each serving contains 12.2 grams of carbohydrate.

1,097 calories in entire recipe; if serving 2, each serving contains 549 calories.

COLESLAW

Makes 4 servings

1 pound cabbage
¼ cup white vinegar
1 tablespoon white wine vinegar
2 tablespoons fresh lemon juice
½ cup sugarless mayonnaise
Artificial sweetener equal to 1 tablespoon sugar
2 tablespoons grated green pepper
2 tablespoons grated sweet red pepper
Salt and pepper to taste

Shred cabbage very fine and place in a large bowl. Add the vinegars, lemon juice, mayonnaise, and artificial sweetener and toss lightly. Mix in the 2 kinds of pepper and add salt and freshly ground black pepper to taste. Place in an attractive serving dish, cover with plastic wrap, and refrigerate until serving time. Coleslaw goes particularly well with fish.

30.4 grams of carbohydrate in entire recipe; if serving 4, each serving contains 7.6 grams of carbohydrate.

919 calories in entire recipe; if serving 4, each serving contains 230 calories.

SWEET-AND-SOUR CUCUMBER SALAD

Serves 4. A refreshing change from the usual tossed salad. Try these cucumbers when serving a rich main course.

2 long, narrow cucumbers
½ cup white vinegar
½ cup cold water
½ teaspoon salt
Dash of black pepper
Artificial sweetener equal to 1 tablespoon sugar

Peel cucumbers and slice as thin as possible. If you get very narrow cucumbers, this can easily be done with a vegetable peeler. Combine vinegar, cold water, salt, pepper, and artificial sweetener and pour this mixture over sliced cucumbers. Marinate overnight in the refrigerator. These cucumbers are particularly good when serving any main dish made with sour cream.

19.2 grams of carbohydrate in entire recipe; if serving 4, each serving contains 4.8 grams of carbohydrate.
70 calories in entire recipe; if serving 4, each serving contains 18 calories.

GREEN BEAN SALAD

Makes 5 servings. A favorite vegetable becomes a salad.

1 pound tiny green beans
2 quarts water
1 tablespoon salt
6 tablespoons olive oil
2 tablespoons mild wine vinegar
3 tablespoons chopped chives, fresh or frozen
Salt
Freshly ground black pepper

Trim the ends from the beans. Bring water to a boil, add salt and beans, return to boil, and cook, uncovered, 8 to 10 minutes. Beans should be crisp-tender. Test 1 by eating it. Set the color by running the beans under cold water, then dry. Mix together oil, vinegar, and chives with salt and pepper to taste. Pour dressing over the beans and refrigerate for at least 2 hours.

29.9 grams of carbohydrate in entire recipe; if serving 5, each serving contains 6.0 grams of carbohydrate.
822 calories in entire recipe; if serving 5, each serving contains 164 calories.

POTATO-LIKE SALAD

Serves 8. I've fooled more people with this recipe. A number of people agreed that this was the best tasting potato salad they had ever eaten, without even knowing there wasn't a potato in it!

2 pounds small white turnips, or larger ones, halved
2 teaspoons salt
2 tablespoons beef broth—may be made with bouillon cube
2 tablespoons dry white wine
6 tablespoons sugarless mayonnaise
2 tablespoons sour cream
4 teaspoons Dijon-style mustard
2 dashes ground celery seed
1 hard-cooked egg
2 tablespoons finely minced onion
2 tablespoons finely minced celery
4 teaspoons finely minced green pepper
4 tablespoons minced parsley
Salt and freshly ground black pepper to taste

Peel the turnips and place in water to cover. Add salt, bring to a boil, lower flame, and cook 20 to 25 minutes until turnips test done with a fork. Remove turnips from the water and dry on paper towels, then cut in small cubes.

Combine the broth and wine and toss turnips with this mixture while still warm. Combine mayonnaise, sour cream, mustard, and celery seed. When the turnips have stood in the wine mixture 10 minutes, add sour cream-mayonnaise, and toss lightly. Dice the hard-cooked egg and add along with the onion, celery, green pepper, and parsley. Lightly toss again. Add salt and pepper to taste. Chill briefly and serve.

57.1 grams of carbohydrate in entire recipe; if serving 8, each serving contains 7.1 grams of carbohydrate.

1,060 calories in entire recipe; if serving 8, each serving contains 134 calories.

NOTE: Potato-like Salad or even real potato salad should never be served icy cold for best flavor. If you are making this in advance, take it out of the refrigerator at least an hour before serving time. See how many people will really believe that they're eating real potato salad if you don't tell them!

FRENCH POTATO-LIKE SALAD

Makes 8 servings. For those who like their potato salad European-style—without mayonnaise.

2 pounds small white turnips, or large ones, halved
2 teaspoons salt
2 tablespoons beef broth—may be made with bouillon cube
2 tablespoons dry white wine
2 tablespoons white wine vinegar
¼ teaspoon salt, dash black pepper
1 teaspoon Dijon-style mustard
6 tablespoons olive oil
2 tablespoons minced scallions
¼ cup minced parsley

Peel the turnips and place in water to cover. Add salt, bring to a boil, lower flame and cook 20 to 25 minutes until the turnips test done with a fork. Remove turnips from the water and dry on paper towels, then cut in thin slices.

Combine the broth and wine and toss the sliced turnips with this mixture while still warm so they will absorb the flavor. Combine vinegar, salt, and mustard and beat to dissolve the salt. Beat in the oil, a little at a time, until all 6 tablespoons are used. Add minced scallions and parsley to the dressing with a dash or two of freshly ground black pepper. Pour the dressing over the turnips and toss lightly to avoid breaking the slices.

55.0 grams of carbohydrate in entire recipe; if serving 8, each serving contains 6.9 grams of carbohydrate.

960 calories in entire recipe; if serving 8, each serving contains 120 calories.

IX.
A VISIT
TO THE ORIENT

A Visit to the Orient

Chinese food is becoming increasingly popular in this country, especially with our warming relationship with Mainland China. Oriental food, when properly prepared, can be low in carbohydrates. Most American Chinese restaurants use far too much cornstarch to thicken their sauces. This extra cornstarch not only adds no flavor and thickens the gravy to a glue-like consistency, it adds unwanted grams of carbohydrates. In China, the food is not thickened to the degree that it is in our restaurants. I have cut down on the amounts of cornstarch customarily used without sacrificing flavor and, more importantly, kept the carbohydrate count low.

In this chapter, I have often purposely omitted mentioning the number of servings for each recipe. Since Chinese food is usually served family-style, with a number of dishes placed on the table to be shared, just add up the carbohydrate and calorie values for each of the dishes you are serving and divide those numbers by the number of people you are serving.

In many of the recipes, I have used the expression *stir-fry* to describe the cooking method for that particular dish. *Stir-fry* is actually another word for *sauté*. In effect, the ingredients are sautéed quickly over high heat, with the food being stirred constantly by holding a pancake turner in one hand and a ladle or basting spoon in the other. The motion is similar to tossing a salad.

Oriental food is a special delight to me and has been one of my favorite things since I was a child. In the section, "Some Useful Ingredients for Low-Carbohydrate Cooking," page 12 at the front of this book, I have included some tips for special Oriental ingredients, which will be helpful to you when you are trying these recipes.

194

CHINESE EGG DROP SOUP

Serves 8. Do you know anybody who doesn't like Chinese Egg Drop Soup? When we were teenagers, my mother would let my sister and me go to the Chinese restaurant by ourselves every Saturday night. How grown-up we felt!

2 eggs
2 teaspoons water
2 scallions
6 cups chicken stock, fresh, canned, or made with a cube
1 teaspoon dry sherry
1 tablespoon Chinese light or Japanese soy sauce
Salt to taste—use less with a packaged broth mix
Artificial sweetener equal to ½ teaspoon sugar

Beat eggs and stir in water. Set aside. Mince scallions and set aside. Bring chicken stock to a boil. Reduce heat to medium and stir in sherry, soy sauce, and salt. Pour eggs in slowly, a little at a time, so that soup continues to boil at all times. Keep stirring constantly, till eggs separate into shreds. A wire whisk is good for this. Remove from heat and stir in artificial sweetener. Garnish with minced scallions.

Any of the following ingredients may be added if desired: soaked, dried black mushrooms, bamboo shoots, lean pork, sesame oil, black pepper, shredded chicken, or 2 more teaspoons dry sherry.

5.0 grams of carbohydrate in entire recipe; if serving 8, each serving contains 0.6 grams of carbohydrate.
403 calories in entire recipe; if serving 8, each serving contains 50 calories.

CHINESE SALAD DRESSING OR SHRIMP DIP

Makes 1 cup plus 2 tablespoons dressing. Even if this mixture sounds odd to you, try it. You'll never be sorry.

6 tablespoons soy sauce
6 tablespoons Chinese rice vinegar, or mild cider or wine vinegar
6 tablespoons Chinese sesame oil
2 teaspoons dry mustard

Combine all ingredients and mix well.

This delightful dressing can be used as a dip for cold shrimp to be served as an appetizer or for Chinese cold salads. If you have never tried a Chinese cold salad, try this on Chinese Chicken Salad (below) and you'll be converted for life.

12.9 grams of carbohydrate in entire recipe; makes 18 tablespoons, each tablespoon containing 0.7 grams of carbohydrate.
759 calories in entire recipe; makes 18 tablespoons, each tablespoon containing 42 calories.

CHINESE CHICKEN SALAD

Makes 8 appetizer servings, or 4 luncheon dish servings. The Chinese certainly can cook, but who would have dreamed of a Chinese chicken salad?

2 whole chicken breasts, cooked
1 large cucumber or 2 small; or
2 stalks celery
½ recipe Chinese Salad Dressing (above)

Using fingers, shred the 2 chicken breasts (the shredding gives texture). Cut up the cucumbers or celery—whichever one you are using—and place on a pretty serving plate. Place shredded chicken on top of cucumbers. Bring the dressing to the table separately and toss the salad with the dressing just before serving.

13.1 grams of carbohydrate in entire recipe if cucumbers are used (10.5 grams if using celery); if serving 8, each serving would contain 1.6 grams (1.3 with celery).

1,129 calories in entire recipe if cucumbers are used (1,111 calories if using celery); if serving 8, each serving would contain 282 calories (278 calories with celery).

CHINESE BEEF AND VEGETABLE SALAD

Makes 4 appetizer servings. Another version of a Chinese cold salad.

2 teaspoons Chinese dark or Japanese soy sauce
2 teaspoons dry sherry
½ teaspoon cornstarch
½ pound beef, sliced very thinly in small strips
2 tablespoons oil
¼ pound cabbage, washed, shredded, and sprinkled with ½ teaspoon salt
¼ pound fresh tomatoes, sliced, then shredded
1 tablespoon soy sauce
1 teaspoon ginger juice
1½ teaspoons Chinese sesame oil

Combine 2 teaspoons soy sauce, sherry, and cornstarch and marinate beef in this mixture 5 minutes. Heat a wok or large frying pan for 30 seconds, add the oil, and heat another 30 seconds over high heat. Add the beef and stir-fry (sauté) until color changes. Remove from pan and cool.

Squeeze any excess water from the cabbage, and arrange on a serving platter in this way: an outside ring of cabbage, the center filled with shredded tomato, and the beef on top of the tomato, leaving a thin ring of tomato showing outside of the meat. Mix the soy sauce, ginger juice, and sesame oil together and place in a small bowl to be taken to the table separately. Toss the salad with the dressing before serving. This salad should be served cold and can be made in advance.

16.2 grams of carbohydrate in entire recipe; if serving 4 as an appetizer, each serving contains 4.1 grams of carbohydrate.

709 calories in entire recipe; if serving 4 as an appetizer, each serving contains 177 calories.

CHINESE STUFFED MUSHROOMS

Makes 4 appetizer servings. If you've never tasted the dried Chinese mushrooms, you're in for a treat. They're marvelously meaty and tasty.

12 large, dried Chinese mushrooms
½ pound very lean ground pork
4 teaspoons Chinese dark or Japanese soy sauce
4 teaspoons very dry sherry
¼ teaspoon salt
Dash of black pepper
1 teaspoon Chinese sesame oil

Soak the mushrooms in warm water for 15 to 30 minutes. Combine ground pork with soy sauce, sherry, salt, pepper, and Chinese sesame oil and mix thoroughly. After mushrooms are softened, remove stems. Divide pork into 12 equal parts. Stuff the mushroom caps with the pork mixture, mounding the tops. Arrange the stuffed mushrooms on a heat-proof plate. Place on a steaming rack and steam for 15 minutes. Serve the stuffed mushrooms with Chinese mustard and/or soy sauce.

14.3 grams of carbohydrate in entire recipe; makes 12 mushrooms, each mushroom containing 1.2 grams of carbohydrate; if serving 4, each serving contains 3.6 grams of carbohydrate.

684 calories in entire recipe; makes 12 mushrooms, each mushroom containing 57 calories; if serving 4, each serving contains 171 calories.

NOTE: To improvise a steamer if you do not have one, place a cake rack in a pot. Place boiling water under the rack, and then place the dish containing the food to be steamed on top of the cake rack. Cover the pot, keeping the flame about medium to avoid burning the pot, and steam the food.

CHINESE STUFFED PEPPERS

Makes 4 appetizer servings

½ pound very lean ground pork or beef
1 extra-large egg
2 teaspoons Chinese dark or Japanese soy sauce
2 teaspoons dry sherry
1 large scallion, minced
½ teaspoon salt
1 slice fresh ginger (1-inch diameter), minced
2 large green peppers, halved
2 tablespoons peanut oil
½ cup water
2 teaspoons Chinese dark or Japanese soy sauce
Granulated artificial sweetener equal to 1 teaspoon sugar

To make the stuffing, mix together meat, egg, soy sauce, sherry, scallion, salt, and ginger. Divide the meat mixture into 4 equal parts and fill each green pepper half, stuffing the meat well into the pepper cavities. Heat a wok or large frying pan 30 seconds, add the oil, heat over high heat for another 30 seconds. Add the peppers, meat side down, and fry 2 minutes, then turn meat-side up and fry 1 minute. Add ½ cup water and 2 teaspoons dark soy sauce and cook over low heat 10 minutes. Remove peppers to a serving platter, raise heat if necessary, and cook down the sauce a little. Remove from heat and stir in artificial sweetener. Pour sauce over peppers and serve hot.

10.5 grams of carbohydrate in entire recipe; if serving 4 as an appetizer, each serving contains 2.6 grams of carbohydrate. The carbohydrate count remains the same whether you use pork or beef.

563 calories in entire recipe if using beef; if serving 4 as an appetizer, each serving contains 141 calories. If using pork, 717 calories in entire recipe; each appetizer serving contains 179 calories.

CHINESE STUFFED CUCUMBERS

Makes 4 appetizer servings. Another version of a stuffed vegetable.

1 very large or 2 small cucumbers
1 recipe stuffing for Chinese Stuffed Peppers (page 199)
2 tablespoons peanut oil
¼ cup chicken stock
2 teaspoons dry sherry
1 teaspoon Chinese dark or Japanese soy sauce
¼ teaspoon salt
Granulated artificial sweetener equal to ½ teaspoon sugar

Peel the cucumbers and cut to make 4 lengthwise sections. Scoop seeds out carefully. Prepare stuffing mix and fill hollowed cucumbers. Heat a wok or frying pan 30 seconds, add the oil, and heat over a high flame another 30 seconds. Add the cucumbers meat-side down. Fry 2 minutes, turning so that sides are cooked evenly. Add sauce ingredients: stock, sherry, soy sauce, and salt. Cook, covered, for 20 minutes.

Remove cucumbers to a serving platter and cook sauce a few more minutes to reduce and/or thicken it. Remove from heat and stir in artificial sweetener. Pour the sauce over cucumbers and serve hot.

11.8 grams of carbohydrate in entire recipe; if serving 4 as an appetizer, each serving contains 3.0 grams of carbohydrate. The carbohydrate count remains the same whether you use pork or beef.

836 calories in entire recipe if using beef; if serving 4 as an appetizer, each serving contains 209 calories. If using pork, 990 calories in entire recipe; each appetizer serving contains 248 calories.

CHINESE STUFFED CABBAGE

Makes 8 cabbage rolls. Every nationality has its stuffed cabbage and here's the Chinese version.

8 leaves Chinese celery cabbage

Stuffing:

½ pound very lean beef, ground
¼ cup finely chopped onion
½ teaspoon salt
2 teaspoons Chinese dark or Japanese soy sauce
2 teaspoons dry sherry

Sauce:

⅓ cup juice from the cabbage after steaming
1 teaspoon Chinese dark or Japanese soy sauce
1 teaspoon Chinese rice vinegar or mild wine or cider vinegar
½ teaspoon cornstarch, mixed with 1 teaspoon cold water
Artificial sweetener equal to 2 teaspoons sugar

Boil the celery cabbage leaves for about 5 minutes, rinse under cold water to stop further cooking, and drain thoroughly. Cut the leaves in 4- to 5-inch sections and reserve the excess trimmings.

Combine ground meat with onion, salt, soy sauce, and sherry

and mix thoroughly. Divide the meat into 8 equal portions, and place 1 in the center of each leaf section. Fold the sides of the leaves over to make neat rolls. Cut the excess trimmings of celery cabbage into ½-inch slices and line a heat-proof bowl with them. Place the cabbage rolls on top. Steam the rolls for 15 minutes, then remove to a serving platter. See Chinese Stuffed Mushrooms (page 198) for directions if you need to improvise a steamer.

Prepare sauce in a small pan, combining ⅓ cup of the juice left after steaming cabbage and add dark soy sauce, rice vinegar, and cornstarch and bring to a boil, stirring constantly. Boil for a few minutes just to thicken sauce a little. Remove from the heat and stir in the artificial sweetener. Pour the sauce over the stuffed cabbage and serve.

14.9 grams of carbohydrate in entire recipe; makes 8 cabbage rolls, each cabbage roll containing 1.9 grams of carbohydrate.

488 calories in entire recipe; makes 8 cabbage rolls, each cabbage roll containing 81 calories.

NOTE: If Chinese celery cabbage is not available, regular round cabbage leaves may be substituted.

DIETETIC CHINESE DUCK SAUCE

Makes 1 cup. A must for Chinese Roast Pork or Chinese Spareribs.

2 ounces sugar-free, artificially sweetened peach jam
3 ounces sugar-free, artificially sweetened apricot jam
1 ounce artificially sweetened strawberry jam
5 tablespoons Chinese rice vinegar (or substitute a mild cider vinegar or a mild wine vinegar)
1 tablespoon minced fresh ginger root
3–4 cloves fresh garlic, crushed

½ teaspoon Chinese dark or Japanese soy sauce
⅛ teaspoon hot red pepper flakes
1 teaspoon chili powder

Combine all ingredients, mix thoroughly, and refrigerate for a few hours or overnight to help develop the flavor. Use as a dip for Chinese food. This sauce keeps well in the refrigerator.

13.9 grams of carbohydrate in entire recipe; makes 1 cup of sauce, each tablespoon containing 0.9 grams of carbohydrate.

118 calories in entire recipe; makes 1 cup of sauce, each tablespoon containing 7 calories.

CHINESE ROAST PORK

Makes 8 appetizer servings, 4 main course servings

2 pounds boneless pork tenderloin
2 tablespoons dry sherry
2 tablespoons dark soy sauce
Brown sugar substitute equal to 2 tablespoons regular brown sugar
1 teaspoon salt
½ teaspoon Chinese 5 Spice Powder°
1 large or 2 small cloves of garlic, minced
2 slices fresh ginger (1-inch diameter), slivered
1 large scallion, cut in 1-inch pieces
Few drops of red food coloring (optional, but nice)

Cut pork into 2 strips lengthwise. Combine remaining ingredients in a shallow bowl or pie plate and mix thoroughly. Place meat in marinade, cover with plastic wrap or foil, refrigerate, and let meat

° NOTE: If you cannot obtain Chinese 5 Spice Powder, you can make it by combining equal parts of powdered cinnamon, powdered cloves, aniseed, and thyme—or substitute ½ teaspoon plain cinnamon.

marinate for at least 3 hours or overnight. Turn meat in the marinade once in a while.

Remove pork strips from marinade. Roast under a hot broiler 1 hour, turning frequently. Baste frequently with the remaining marinade. May be eaten hot or cold with Chinese mustard or Dietetic Chinese Duck Sauce (page 202).

8.2 grams of carbohydrate in entire recipe; if serving 8 as an appetizer, each serving contains 1.0 grams of carbohydrate. If serving 4 as a main course, each serving contains 2.0 grams of carbohydrate.

2,392 calories in entire recipe; if serving 8 as an appetizer, each serving contains 299 calories. If serving 4 as a main course, each serving contains 598 calories.

CHINESE PORK AND CUCUMBERS

½ pound lean pork
Marinade of 2 teaspoons soy sauce, ½ teaspoon cornstarch, and 1 teaspoon dry sherry
2 cups sliced large cucumbers, or whole small pickling cucumbers
2 tablespoons peanut oil
1 tablespoon soy sauce
Artificial sweetener equal to ½ teaspoon sugar
Dash of salt

Cut the pork into very thin slices or tiny cubes. Place in marinade for 5 minutes. Wash cucumbers; if large, peel, seed, and slice at a diagonal; if small pickling variety, dry and use whole without peeling. Heat a wok or large frying pan, add oil, wait about 30 seconds, then add pork. Stir-fry the pork over high heat until the color changes. Add the remaining ingredients and continue to stir-fry for another 1 to 2 minutes. Serve hot.

10.9 grams of carbohydrate in entire recipe.
774 calories in entire recipe.

CHINESE BARBECUED SPARERIBS

Makes 6 appetizer servings. An old favorite of my childhood Chinese restaurant days.

One 2-pound rack of spareribs
2 tablespoons Chinese dark or Japanese soy sauce
2 tablespoons very dry sherry
2 tablespoons sugar-free, artificially sweetened, orange marmalade
2 tablespoons sugar-free, artificially sweetened, strawberry jam
1 teaspoon salt
4 slices fresh ginger (1-inch diameter), minced
4 large cloves of garlic, minced
2 scallions, cut in 1-inch pieces
Few drops red food coloring (optional, but nice)

If possible, try to obtain small spareribs. Do not separate them; leave them as a rack; but have the butcher crack the bones. Combine remaining ingredients, mix well, and marinate the spareribs in this mixture. For convenience, use a large plastic bag and turn the entire bag over to turn the spareribs in the marinade. Place a plate underneath the plastic bag in case any of the liquid leaks. Marinate ribs at least 4 hours or overnight, turning occasionally.

Preheat oven to 350° F. Separate ribs, place in a shallow roasting pan (I like to use a disposable pan) and bake 1 hour and 15 minutes, basting frequently with any remaining marinade. The spareribs should now be browned; if not, turn oven up to 475° F. for 5 or 10 minutes. Serve with Chinese mustard or Dietetic Chinese Duck Sauce (page 202).

11.0 grams of carbohydrate in entire recipe; if serving 6 as an appetizer, each serving contains 1.8 grams of carbohydrate.

2,068 calories in entire recipe; if serving 6 as an appetizer, each serving contains 345 calories.

CHINESE BEEF AND BROCCOLI

Chinese meals are both quick and delicious. This recipe even uses convenient frozen broccoli.

¾ pound flank steak
2 tablespoons soy sauce
1 tablespoon dry sherry
½ teaspoon cornstarch
1 package frozen broccoli, defrosted
1 clove garlic, minced
1 thin slice fresh ginger (1-inch diameter), finely minced
2 tablespoons peanut oil
Salt to taste

Slice the steak against the grain into very thin slices. Combine the soy sauce, sherry, and cornstarch and pour this mixture over the steak. Marinate the meat for 15 minutes.

While the meat is marinating, slice the broccoli at a diagonal and mince garlic and ginger. Heat a wok or large frying pan for 30 seconds, add oil, wait about 20 seconds, and add minced garlic and ginger root. Fry over high heat, stirring constantly for about 20 seconds more, then add the beef. Stir-fry, stirring constantly, for about 1 minute. Add broccoli and stir-fry for another 4 to 6 minutes, until the broccoli is cooked but still crisp and still dark green. Serve hot.

18.4 grams of carbohydrate in entire recipe.
864 calories in entire recipe.

CHINESE BEEF AND ASPARAGUS

If you thought that the only way to eat asparagus was with hollandaise, this may surprise you.

¾ pound flank steak
1½ tablespoons soy sauce
1 teaspoon dry sherry
Granulated artificial sweetener equal to ½ teaspoon sugar
½ teaspoon cornstarch
2 tablespoons peanut oil
½ pound fresh asparagus (see NOTE)
1 tablespoon shredded scallion
¼ teaspoon salt, or to taste

Slice the steak against the grain in very thin slices. (This is easily done by slicing the meat when it is slightly frozen.) Combine the soy sauce, sherry, artificial sweetener, and cornstarch and pour this mixture over beef. Marinate the steak 15 minutes.

While the meat is marinating, trim off the tough lower end of asparagus stalks and slice asparagus at a diagonal. Boil 1 cup of water, drop asparagus into it, and when water returns to boil, cook 2 minutes. Drain the asparagus.

Heat a wok or large frying pan for 30 seconds, add oil, count to 30, add scallion and beef, and stir-fry over high heat about 1 minute. Add asparagus and salt and continue to stir-fry for 2 more minutes.

10.7 grams of carbohydrate in entire recipe.
806 calories in entire recipe.

NOTE: You may substitute one package of frozen asparagus if fresh is not available. Then do not boil, merely defrost.

CHINESE PEPPER STEAK

¾ pound lean beef
Marinade of 2 teaspoons soy sauce, artificial sweetener equal to ½
    teaspoon sugar, 1 teaspoon dry sherry, and ½ teaspoon cornstarch
1½ green peppers
½ red pepper
1 slice fresh ginger (1-inch diameter)
2 tablespoons peanut oil
1 tablespoon soy sauce mixed with 1 teaspoon dry sherry

Slice the beef into thin strips and place in marinade for 15 minutes.

While the meat is marinating, slice peppers thinly and mince the ginger. Mix together the seasonings and set aside.

Heat a wok or large frying pan for 30 seconds, add 1 tablespoon of the oil, continue heating for another 30 seconds over high heat. Add the peppers and stir-fry 2 minutes. Remove peppers to a warm plate.

Add the remaining tablespoon of oil to the wok, heat 30 seconds more, add the ginger, and heat until golden brown. Add beef and stir-fry until the color of beef changes. Return peppers to the pan, add soy-sherry seasoning and continue to stir-fry for another minute or 2 until all ingredients are thoroughly mixed. Serve hot.

10.9 grams of carbohydrate in entire recipe.
815 calories in entire recipe.

BEEF WITH CHINESE VEGETABLES

½ pound lean beef
Marinade of 1 teaspoon soy sauce, 1 teaspoon dry sherry, and ½
    teaspoon cornstarch
1 clove garlic, minced
1 slice fresh ginger, minced

4 dried Chinese mushrooms, soaked 30 minutes in warm water
6–8 snow peas, stringed
3 water chestnuts, each sliced in 3 slices
¼ cup bamboo shoots, sliced

Seasonings Mixture:

2 teaspoons soy sauce
2 teaspoons dry sherry
Artificial sweetener equal to ½ teaspoon sugar
2 tablespoons peanut oil

Slice the beef into thin strips and place in marinade 15 minutes.

While the meat is marinating, mince the garlic and ginger, slice the mushrooms into thin strips, string the snow peas, and slice the water chestnuts. Mix together the seasonings. Heat a wok or large frying pan for 30 seconds, add 1 tablespoon of oil, and continue heating for another 30 seconds over high heat. Add the vegetables and stir-fry for 2 minutes. Remove them to a warm plate.

Add the remaining tablespoon of oil, heat 30 seconds more, add the meat, and stir-fry until meat changes color. Return the vegetables to the pan, add seasoning mixture and blend thoroughly. Cook for 1 or 2 minutes more until thoroughly combined. Serve hot.

15.8 grams of carbohydrate in entire recipe.
670 calories in entire recipe.

CHINESE CHICKEN AND CAULIFLOWER

Definitely one of the fastest yet most delicious ways of preparing chicken that I've ever tasted.

1 skinless, boneless chicken breast (about 8 ounces)
2 tablespoons soy sauce
1 tablespoon dry sherry
Granulated artificial sweetener equal to 1 teaspoon sugar

½ teaspoon cornstarch
3 tablespoons minced cooked ham
1 tablespoon Chinese parsley (regular parsley may be substituted)
1 package frozen cauliflower, defrosted
2 tablespoons peanut oil
2 tablespoons water
Salt to taste

Cut the raw chicken breast in thin slices. Combine the soy sauce, sherry, artificial sweetener, and cornstarch and pour over chicken. Marinate the chicken in this mixture 10 minutes.

While chicken is marinating, chop ham and parsley. Pour boiling water over cauliflower, leave 1 minute, drain, and set aside.

Heat a wok or large frying pan for 30 seconds, add the oil, count to 30, and add chicken slices. Stir-fry chicken over high heat for about 2 minutes. Add cauliflower and continue stir-frying another 2 minutes. Add water and salt to taste and cover tightly. Cook 5 minutes. Remove to a serving dish, and sprinkle parsley and ham on top.

13.1 grams of carbohydrate in entire recipe.
750 calories in entire recipe.

CHINESE CHICKEN AND PEPPERS

1 skinless, boneless chicken breast (about 8 ounces)
Marinade of 1 teaspoon dry sherry and ½ teaspoon cornstarch
1½ green peppers
½ red pepper
1 tablespoon dry sherry
½ teaspoon salt
Granulated artificial sweetener equal to ½ teaspoon sugar
3 tablespoons peanut oil

Slice the chicken breast into thin slices. Marinate the chicken in sherry and cornstarch for 5 minutes. Halve the peppers, seed, and slice into very thin slices. Combine 1 tablespoon of sherry, ½ tea-spoon salt, and the artificial sweetener and set aside.

Heat a wok or large frying pan for 30 seconds, add 1 tablespoon of the oil, wait 30 seconds, add peppers and stir-fry for 2 minutes. Remove peppers to a plate. Add remaining 2 tablespoons of oil, and stir-fry chicken until it turns white. Return the peppers to pan, add the seasonings mixed earlier and continue to stir-fry until all ingredients are well mixed (about 1 minute). Serve immediately.

7.9 grams of carbohydrate in entire recipe.
821 calories in entire recipe.

CHINESE SHRIMP EGG FOO YONG

Makes 8 pancakes

Sauce:

¾ cup chicken broth
1 tablespoon soy sauce
½ teaspoon cornstarch
Additional salt if desired

Pancakes:

½ pound shrimp, shelled and deveined
¼ pound fresh mushrooms
3 extra-large eggs
1 tablespoon peanut oil
½ cup bean sprouts
¼ teaspoon salt
1 teaspoon dry sherry
Artificial sweetener equal to ¼ teaspoon sugar
1½ tablespoons additional peanut oil

To make the sauce, bring the chicken broth to a boil. Add soy sauce and cornstarch. Boil 1 to 2 minutes until sauce turns clear and thickens slightly. Keep warm over very low heat while you make pancakes.

Dice the shrimp and mushrooms into ¼-inch pieces. Beat the eggs in a bowl. Heat a wok or frying pan for 30 seconds, add 1 tablespoon of the oil, and continue heating for another 30 seconds. Add shrimp and stir-fry until pink. Add the sautéed shrimp to the eggs, then add the mushrooms and bean sprouts to the eggs along with salt, sherry, and artificial sweetener.

Brush the bottom of the same wok or of a 5- or 6-inch frying pan with 1 teaspoon oil, reduce flame to low, and pour in approximately ¼ cup of the egg-shrimp batter. Allow it to cook for 1 minute without touching it. When lightly browned (you may peek), turn it, and cook another minute or so until that side is lightly browned, too. Remove to a warm plate and cover with aluminum foil to keep warm. Repeat until all 8 pancakes are made, brushing the pan with ½ teaspoon oil before making each new pancake. Serve these pancakes hot with the sauce spooned over them.

14.4 grams of carbohydrate in entire recipe; makes 8 pancakes, each pancake contains 1.8 grams of carbohydrate.

822 calories in entire recipe; makes 8 pancakes, each pancake contains 103 calories.

CHINESE BARBECUED SHRIMP AND LIVERS

Makes 4 servings

1 pound large shrimp, shelled and deveined
5 strips bacon
½ pound chicken livers
½ clove garlic
2 slices fresh ginger (1-inch diameter)
½ cup soy sauce

¼ cup dry sherry
½ teaspoon salt
Dash of pepper
Granulated artificial sweetener equal to 1½ tablespoons sugar

Butterfly the shrimp. Cut each bacon strip into 4 pieces. Cut each chicken liver in half. Arrange the flattened shrimp in a dish. Place a piece of chicken liver on each shrimp, then top each piece of liver with a piece of the bacon. Mince the garlic and ginger root. Combine soy sauce, sherry, salt, pepper, and artificial sweetener with the ginger and garlic. Pour over the shrimp and let stand for 20 to 30 minutes. Thread skewers with the shrimp, chicken livers, and bacon in layers. Broil or barbecue the skewers, turning frequently until the shrimp turn pink.

23.4 grams of carbohydrate in entire recipe; if serving 4, each serving contains 5.9 grams of carbohydrate.
918 calories in entire recipe; if serving 4, each serving contains 240 calories.

CHINESE SHRIMP WITH CUCUMBERS

1 pound uncooked shrimp, shelled and deveined
1 teaspoon dry sherry
2 teaspoons salt
Granulated artificial sweetener equal to 1 teaspoon sugar
½ teaspoon cornstarch
2 medium cucumbers or 3 small pickling cucumbers
2 tablespoons peanut oil
1 tablespoon additional dry sherry

Wash and dry shrimp. Mix together the sherry, salt, artificial sweetener and cornstarch, and marinate the shrimp in this mixture 15 minutes. While the shrimp are marinating, prepare cucumbers: if small pickling variety, just wash and dry; if larger ones, peel, seed, and quarter lengthwise. Slice cucumbers in 1-inch slices.

Heat a wok or large frying pan for 30 seconds, add 1 tablespoon of oil, wait 30 seconds more, add cucumbers, and stir-fry until slightly transparent (3 to 5 minutes). Remove cucumbers to a plate. Add remaining oil and stir-fry the shrimp until pink. Return cucumbers to the pan, add additional sherry and continue to stir-fry for another 2 minutes. Serve hot.

20.3 grams of carbohydrate in entire recipe.
751 calories in entire recipe.

CHINESE SHRIMP WITH PEPPERS AND MUSHROOMS

½ pound shrimp, shelled and deveined
½ teaspoon ginger juice (page 16)
½ teaspoon cornstarch
½ cup green peppers, cut in ½-inch squares
½ cup fresh mushrooms, cut in ½-inch squares

Seasonings Mixture:

2 teaspoons dry sherry
½ teaspoon salt
Granulated artificial sweetener equal to 1 teaspoon sugar
2 tablespoons peanut oil

Marinate shrimp 5 minutes in the ginger juice and cornstarch. Meanwhile, cut the peppers and mushrooms. Combine the seasonings and set aside.

Heat a wok over high heat for 30 seconds, then add oil, wait another 30 seconds for the oil to become very hot, and stir-fry the shrimp until bright pink. Add the peppers and mushrooms and stir-fry for another 2 minutes. Add the seasonings mixed earlier and continue to stir-fry for another 2 or 3 minutes.

9.9 grams of carbohydrate in entire recipe.
505 calories in entire recipe.

CHINESE SHRIMP AND BROCCOLI

Follow recipe for Chinese Shrimp with Peppers and Mushrooms (page 214), substituting half a package of frozen broccoli, defrosted in advance, for the peppers and mushrooms. Slice the broccoli stems in diagonal slices and separate the flowerets into mouth-size pieces.

12.7 grams of carbohydrate in entire recipe.
520 calories in entire recipe.

JAPANESE GRILLED BEEF

Makes 3 servings. In Japan, they hand-tend their cattle for their famous Kobe beef to make this dish.

⅓ cup Japanese soy sauce
1 tablespoon sake or dry sherry
Artificial sweetener equal to 4½ tablespoons sugar
1 small clove of garlic, minced
1½ pounds lean beef sirloin or tenderloin, sliced ½-inch thick
2 teaspoons peanut oil
3 green peppers, each cut vertically in 3 pieces

Mix together the soy sauce, sake, artificial sweetener, and garlic. Marinate the beef in this mixture 15 minutes. Brush a heavy griddle or frying pan with the oil. Grill the beef and peppers until done to taste. Cook peppers alone first if you like your meat rare. If you have an outdoor grill, try this on it.

17.1 grams of carbohydrate in entire recipe; if serving 3, each serving contains 5.7 grams of carbohydrate.
1,669 calories in entire recipe; if serving 3, each serving contains 417 calories.

SUKIYAKI

Makes 5 to 6 servings

1 cup beef stock
½ cup sake or dry sherry
5 tablespoons Japanese soy sauce
Artificial sweetener equal to ½ cup sugar
2 pounds lean beef sirloin or tenderloin, sliced paper thin
¾ pound mushrooms, thinly sliced
8 scallions, cut in 2-inch lengths
1 pound Chinese celery cabbage, sliced in ½-inch rounds
4 cakes bean curd, cut in 1-inch cubes (baked bean curd preferred)
1 tablespoon peanut oil

Combine in a small bowl or pitcher the beef stock, sake, soy sauce, and artificial sweetener and set aside. This is the sauce that the other ingredients will be cooked in.

Slice the beef into paper-thin slices. (This is more easily done if the meat is partially frozen.) Have 2 large trays ready and arrange half the meat on each tray. Divide in the same way the sliced mushrooms, scallions, celery cabbage, and bean curd cubes. Form a decorative design with the different ingredients as you arrange them; Japanese people give a great deal of attention to making their food look beautiful.

Sukiyaki is customarily cooked at the table with a little of the ingredients added at a time. Have ready an electric skillet or a small electric 1-burner stove that can be brought to the table with a wide heavy casserole. Oil the pan thoroughly with the peanut oil. Cover the pan bottom with a few beef slices and brown them on both sides. Push the meat to 1 side, then add some of each of the vegetables and some cooking sauce. Continue cooking over low heat. Serve the food and eat it while you cook more. Just add more beef, vegetables, bean curd, and sauce as the food is removed. Serve green tea in small Japanese cups with the Sukiyaki.

55.5 grams of carbohydrate in entire recipe; if serving 6, each serving contains 9.3 grams of carbohydrate.

2,843 calories in entire recipe; if serving 6, each serving contains 474 calories.

X.
SAUCES, DRESSINGS
& TOPPINGS:
A FEW LITTLE THINGS

Sauces, Dressings & Toppings: A Few Little Things

Here are a variety of sauces, salad dressings, and toppings for sweet things. These are what dress up your cooking and can make the difference between the ordinary and the extraordinary.

WHITE SAUCE

Makes 1 cup. Use this white sauce whenever a recipe calls for regular white sauce.

2 tablespoons butter
2 tablespoons full-fat soy flour
½ cup heavy cream
½ cup cold water
Salt to taste
Dash of white pepper
2 egg yolks

Melt butter in a heavy saucepan over low heat. With a wire whisk, stir in soy flour, and cook a few minutes until thoroughly blended. Combine cream and water and add slowly to the butter-flour mixture, stirring constantly with the wire whisk. Add salt and pepper to taste. Heat to scalding, then beat in egg yolks, 1 at a time. Do not allow mixture to boil.

8.3 grams of carbohydrate in entire recipe; makes 1 cup of sauce, each tablespoon containing 0.5 grams of carbohydrate.

803 calories in entire recipe; makes 1 cup of sauce, each tablespoon containing 50 calories.

SPICED CRANBERRY SAUCE

Makes approximately 3 cups. A low-carbohydrate sauce to serve with turkey.

One 1-pound box fresh cranberries
1½ cups water
2 teaspoons freshly grated orange peel
Dash of allspice
Dash of cloves
10 drops orange extract
Artificial sweetener equal to 2 cups sugar

Bring cranberries, water, and orange peel to a boil. Boil until the skin of the berries pops open (about 5 minutes). Remove from heat, add remaining ingredients, and mix till thoroughly combined. Cool in refrigerator before serving.

43.2 grams of carbohydrate in entire recipe; makes approximately 3 cups, each tablespoon containing 0.9 grams of carbohydrate.

235 calories in entire recipe; makes approximately 3 cups, each tablespoon containing 5 calories.

APRICOT SAUCE FOR DUCK OR CHICKEN

Makes approximately 2⅜ cups. Apricot sauce makes a nice change from the usual orange sauce for duck.

2 cups sugar-free, artificially sweetened apricot jam
1 teaspoon minced fresh ginger root
¼ cup dry sherry
Dash of cardamom
2 dashes cloves
Dash of allspice
2 tablespoons Grand Marnier
⅛ teaspoon minced garlic
Artificial sweetener equal to 1 cup sugar

In a heavy saucepan, combine the jam, ginger root, sherry, cardamom, cloves, allspice, Grand Marnier, and garlic. Heat over a low flame, stirring frequently until all flavors are thoroughly combined and mixture comes to a boil. Remove from heat and add artificial sweetener. Allow the mixture to stand for 10 to 15 minutes before serving to allow it to thicken again. Spoon the sauce over roasted or barbecued duck or chicken.

17.4 grams of carbohydrate in entire recipe; makes approximately 2⅜ cups of sauce, each tablespoon containing 0.5 grams of carbohydrate.
260 calories in entire recipe; makes approximately 2⅜ cups of sauce, each tablespoon containing 7 calories.

CHERRY SAUCE FOR DUCK OR CHICKEN

Makes approximately 1¼ cups of sauce. A dietetic version of sauce for Duck Montmorency.

1 cup sugar-free, artificially sweetened cherry jam
1½ teaspoons minced fresh ginger root
1 tablespoon Cognac or other good brandy

3 tablespoons dry sherry
1 tablespoon fresh lemon juice
Dash of cloves
Dash of cardamom
Dash of coriander
Artificial sweetener equal to 6 tablespoons sugar

In a heavy saucepan, combine the jam, ginger root, Cognac, sherry, lemon juice, cloves, cardamom, and coriander. Heat over low flame stirring frequently until all flavors are thoroughly combined and mixture comes to a boil. Remove from heat, add artificial sweetener and wait about 10 minutes before you serve the sauce. This will give the melted liquid a chance to thicken again. Spoon the sauce over roasted or barbecued duck or chicken.

6.2 grams of carbohydrate in entire recipe; makes approximately 1¼ cups of sauce, each tablespoon containing 0.3 grams of carbohydrate.
141 calories in entire recipe; makes approximately 1¼ cups of sauce, each tablespoon containing 7.0 calories.

PEACH SAUCE FOR DUCK OR CHICKEN

Makes approximately 1 cup

1 cup sugarless peach jam
1 tablespoon dry sherry
1 teaspoon fresh lime juice
Granulated artificial sweetener equal to ½ cup sugar

In a heavy saucepan, combine the jam, dry sherry, and lime juice. Heat over a low flame, stirring frequently, until all flavors are thoroughly combined and mixture comes to a boil. Remove from heat and add artificial sweetener. Allow to stand for 10 or 15 minutes before serving to give the melted liquid a chance to thicken again. Spoon the sauce over roasted or barbecued duck or chicken.

4.7 grams of carbohydrate in entire recipe; makes approximately 1 cup, each tablespoon containing 0.3 grams of carbohydrate.

55 calories in entire recipe; makes approximately 1 cup, each tablespoon containing 3 calories.

MINT JELLY

Makes approximately 1¾ cups. A must for lamb.

½ cup fresh mint leaves
1 cup boiling water
1 envelope unflavored gelatin
½ cup cold water
⅓ cup fresh lime juice
Artificial sweetener equal to ¼ cup sugar
4–5 drops green food coloring

Crush mint leaves, then pour boiling water over them. Cover the dish and allow to stand for 5 minutes. Meanwhile, soften the gelatin in cold water for 5 minutes. Strain the mint liquid into the softened gelatin and stir until the gelatin dissolves completely. Add ⅓ cup fresh lime juice, artificial sweetener, and enough green food coloring to make a pretty shade of green. Mix thoroughly, then pour the mixture into a 2-cup mold or pretty serving dish and chill thoroughly.

7.4 grams of carbohydrate in entire recipe; makes approximately 1¾ cups of jelly, each tablespoon containing 0.3 grams of carbohydrate.

49 calories in entire recipe; makes approximately 1¾ cups of jelly, each tablespoon containing 2 calories.

MINT SAUCE

Makes approximately 1 cup. Try Mint Sauce instead of Mint Jelly with lamb.

1 cup fresh mint leaves
¼ cup boiling water
⅓ cup mild wine vinegar
Artificial sweetener equal to 3 tablespoons sugar

Wash and dry the mint leaves, then chop finely. Place in a bowl and add boiling water. Mix in the vinegar and artificial sweetener. Allow the mixture to stand for at least 2 hours, preferably longer for flavor to develop and blend. Try serving this sauce with lamb chops or leg of lamb.

4.2 grams of carbohydrate in entire recipe; makes approximately 1 cup of
   sauce, each tablespoon containing 0.3 grams of carbohydrate.
11 calories in entire recipe; makes approximately 1 cup of sauce, each
   tablespoon containing 0.7 calorie (less than 1 calorie per tablespoon).

CURRY SAUCE FOR SEAFOOD

Makes 1 cup. This makes a pleasant change from the usual sauces for cold seafood.

¾ cup sugarless mayonnaise
2 tablespoons heavy cream
2 tablespoons cold water
1 tablespoon Madras curry powder (page 15)
Dash of garlic powder

Combine all ingredients and beat with an electric mixer or a wire whisk until smooth and well blended. Use as a sauce for cold shrimp, lobster, or crabmeat.

8.1 grams of carbohydrate in entire recipe; makes 1 cup of sauce, each tablespoon containing 0.5 grams of carbohydrate.

1,336 calories in entire recipe; makes 1 cup of sauce, each tablespoon containing 84 calories.

DILLED SHRIMP SAUCE

Makes approximately 1 cup. This sauce is the highlight of the meal any time I serve it.

¼ cup sugarless mayonnaise
¼ cup sour cream
¼ cup chili sauce
1½ teaspoons freshly grated onion
6 tablespoons chopped fresh dill
Generous amount freshly ground black pepper

Beat the mayonnaise until very smooth and softened. I generally use a glass measuring cup to make this. You measure and make it in the same cup that way. Beat in the sour cream and when thoroughly blended, beat in the chili sauce. Mix in the remaining ingredients in the above order. Allow the sauce to sit for a few hours before serving.

To use as a sauce for shrimp cocktails, arrange fresh, cooked and cooled shrimp around the dish and place about a tablespoon of the sauce in the center. When used as part of an hors d'oeuvre tray, pour some of the sauce over the shrimp before bringing it to the table. This sauce is also good as a party dip for dipping raw vegetables.

18.6 grams of carbohydrate in entire recipe; makes 1 cup, each tablespoon containing 1.2 grams of carbohydrate.

581 calories in entire recipe; makes 1 cup, each tablespoon containing 36 calories.

GARLIC & PARSLEY SAUCE FOR SHRIMP

Makes ½ cup. How about cold Scampi?

¼ cup olive oil
1½ tablespoons white wine vinegar
1 tablespoon fresh lemon juice
2 tablespoons finely minced parsley, preferably Italian parsley if
    available
¼ teaspoon salt, or more to taste
⅛ teaspoon dry mustard
1 large clove garlic, minced or put through a press
Generous dash freshly ground black pepper

Combine all ingredients and shake well to blend. Use as a sauce for
shrimp cocktails. Arrange the shrimp prettily on a lettuce leaf and
spoon some of the sauce over them.

3.2 grams of carbohydrate in entire recipe; makes 8 tablespoons, each
    tablespoon containing 0.4 grams of carbohydrate.
506 calories in entire recipe; makes 8 tablespoons, each tablespoon
    containing 63 calories.

MAYONNAISE VERTE

Makes approximately 2½ cups. Cold poached salmon without this
sauce is nothing.

2 whole eggs
Juice of 1 lemon
1 large or 2 small cloves of fresh garlic
¾ teaspoon dry mustard
¾ teaspoon salt
2 cups olive oil
¼ cup minced chives, fresh or frozen

20 large spinach leaves, coarsely chopped
¼ cup watercress leaves
½ cup fresh parsley
1 heaping tablespoon fresh tarragon or 2 teaspoons dried tarragon

Place in a blender the eggs, lemon juice, garlic, dry mustard, and salt. Cover the container and blend at high speed till thoroughly mixed. Remove the feeder cap and slowly add the oil in a steady stream, continuing to run the blender at highest speed. Remove the cover, add the remaining ingredients, re-cover, and continue to blend until all the greens are thoroughly incorporated into the mixture. Remove to a storage container, and chill in refrigerator until serving time.

10 grams of carbohydrate in entire recipe; each tablespoon contains 0.3 grams of carbohydrate.
3,814 calories in entire recipe; each tablespoon contains 95 calories.

NOTE: This sauce is marvelous served with cold poached salmon, but can be served deliciously with any cold seafood—shrimp, lobster, crabmeat, et al.

CREAMY MUSTARD SAUCE

Makes 1½ cups. A delightful sauce for cold seafood.

½ cup sugarless mayonnaise
½ cup sour cream
¼ cup Dijon-style mustard
¼ cup chopped fresh dill

Beat mayonnaise until very smooth and softened. Beat in the sour cream and when thoroughly blended, beat in the mustard. Fold in the chopped dill. Keep this sauce in the refrigerator for a few hours to blend the flavors and develop them. Use sauce for cold seafood such as shrimp, lobster, scallops, or crabmeat.

11.6 grams of carbohydrate in entire recipe; makes 1½ cups of sauce, each tablespoon containing 0.5 grams of carbohydrate.

1,120 calories in entire recipe; makes 1½ cups of sauce, each tablespoon containing 47 calories.

CHEESE SAUCE

Makes 1 cup. Try this cheese sauce over freshly steamed vegetables.

1 recipe White Sauce
¼ cup (1 ounce) grated sharp Cheddar cheese
Dash of cayenne pepper
Dash of nutmeg

Follow ingredients and method for White Sauce (page 218), adding the grated cheese, cayenne pepper, and nutmeg before adding egg yolks. Allow cheese to melt, then beat in the yolks.

8.9 grams of carbohydrate in entire recipe; makes 1 cup of sauce, each tablespoon containing 0.6 grams of carbohydrate.

918 calories in entire recipe; makes 1 cup of sauce, each tablespoon containing 57 calories.

VINAIGRETTE DRESSING

Makes 1 cup. This is the true French dressing.

¾ cup good quality olive oil
¼ cup good quality mild wine vinegar
½ teaspoon salt
Generous sprinkling of freshly ground black pepper
1 clove garlic (optional)

Combine all ingredients in a blender and blend at high speed just until thoroughly combined.

3.0 grams of carbohydrate in entire recipe; makes 1 cup, each tablespoon containing 0.2 grams of carbohydrate.

1,399 calories in entire recipe; makes 1 cup, each tablespoon containing 87 calories.

BEACH HOUSE MUSTARD DRESSING

Makes 1 cup. This dressing was taught to me by a French girl who visited our beach house in Southampton. It became the favorite of the house.

¼ cup brown mustard
¾ cup olive oil
1 tablespoon vinegar
Few dashes of garlic salt
Few dashes of ground celery seed
Few dashes of freshly ground black pepper

Place the mustard in a medium-sized bowl. Add garlic salt, ground celery seed, and pepper. Very slowly with a wire whisk or electric mixer, beat in the oil a little at a time, as if you were making mayonnaise. Do not add more oil until the previous amount is thoroughly blended in or this sauce will curdle. Keep adding oil, mixing it in thoroughly until all oil is used up and the dressing looks like a thick mayonnaise. Beat it in the vinegar to thin it a little. Serve over Salade Niçoise (page 186) or over any tossed green salad.

6.8 grams of carbohydrate in entire recipe; makes 16 tablespoons, each tablespoon containing 0.4 grams of carbohydrate.

1,478 calories in entire recipe; makes 16 tablespoons, each tablespoon containing 92 calories.

ROQUEFORT DRESSING

Makes approximately 1½ cups. A delight with a green salad.

¾ cup good quality olive oil
¼ cup good quality mild wine vinegar
¼ pound imported French Roquefort cheese, crumbled
Salt and pepper to taste

Beat the oil and vinegar until an emulsion is formed. Mash in the Roquefort cheese and mix thoroughly. Add salt and freshly ground black pepper to taste. You can crumble additional Roquefort cheese into the salad if you desire.

5.0 grams of carbohydrate in entire recipe; makes approximately 1½ cups, each tablespoon containing 0.2 grams of carbohydrate.
1,819 calories in entire recipe; makes approximately 1½ cups, each tablespoon containing 65 calories.

CINNAMON-SUGAR TOPPING

Makes ½ cup. Use this in place of cinnamon-sugar and you'll barely know the difference.

Granulated sugar substitute, equal to ½ cup sugar
1 teaspoon cinnamon

Mix artificial sweetener and cinnamon until well combined. Store in a glass jar or plastic container to use as desired.

9.1 grams of carbohydrate in entire recipe; makes ½ cup, each teaspoon containing 0.4 grams of carbohydrate.
36 calories in entire recipe; makes ½ cup, each teaspoon containing 1.5 calories.

NUTTED CHEESE SPREAD

Makes 24 tablespoons. Try this with Cinnamon Bread.

One 8-ounce package whipped cream cheese
⅓ cup walnuts, coarsely chopped

Allow the cream cheese to stand for about 20 minutes to soften at room temperature. Mix in the walnuts thoroughly. Store in a covered dish in the refrigerator.

9.6 grams of carbohydrate in entire recipe; makes 24 tablespoons, each tablespoon containing 0.4 grams of carbohydrate.
1,053 calories in entire recipe; makes 24 tablespoons, each tablespoon containing 44 calories.

CARBOHYDRATE GRAM & CALORIE COUNTING CHARTS

Carbohydrate Gram & Calorie Counting Charts

All foods are not equal in the degree to which they will make you gain weight, even if they have the same carbohydrate and/or calorie values.

A team of doctors, headed by Dr. Walton W. Shreeve at Brookhaven National Laboratory, conducted studies which showed that when patients were fed diets that were alternately high in sugar and starch content, the percentage of sugar converted to blood fat was 2 to 5 percent higher than the percentage of starch converted to blood fat.

This research suggests that any simple carbohydrate food (sugar) is two to five times as fattening as a complex carbohydrate food (starch). Therefore, food containing sugar is two to five times as fattening as food containing starch, even though their carbohydrate gram values may be similar or their calorie amounts equal.

NOTE: Figures in the accompanying charts were compiled from the Department of Agriculture Handbook No. 8, *Composition of Foods* (Washington: United States Department of Agriculture, 1963) and *The Dictionary of Calories & Carbohydrates* by Barbara Kraus (New York: Grosset & Dunlap, 1973). The letters n.d.a. following an entry mean no data available.

CARBOHYDRATES AND CALORIES
IN INGREDIENTS USED IN THIS BOOK

° ° These items are relatively high in carbohydrate value. Use them sparingly.

Food and Quantity	Carbo- hydrate Grams	Calories
ALMONDS, slivered, 1 tbl.	2.1	63
ANCHOVY PASTE, 1 tbl.	1.0	20
ARTICHOKE HEARTS, frozen, ⅓ pkg.	4.8	22
BACON, cured, broiled or fried crisp, drained		
1 thick slice	0.4	73
1 thin slice	0.2	31
BACON, CANADIAN, unheated, 1 oz.	trace	61
BAKING POWDER, phosphate, 1 teas.	1.4	6
BAMBOO SHOOTS, canned, sliced, ½ cup	1.0	6
BEAN CURD, Chinese, 1 cake (4.2 oz.)	2.9	86
BEAN SPROUTS, canned (La Choy), 1 cup	1.0	15
Fresh, raw, Mung, 4 oz.	7.5	40
Fresh, raw, soy, 4 oz.	6.0	52
BEANS, green or snap, fresh, 4 oz. weighed untrimmed	7.1	32
BEEF		
Flank, raw, 100% lean, 4 oz.	0	163
Filet mignon. There are no data available currently, but for the closest possible approximation, use the figures for sirloin steak, lean only.		
Ground, raw, lean, 4 oz.	0	203
Rib steak or roast, roasted or broiled, lean only, boneless, 4 oz.	0	273

233

Food and Quantity	Carbo-hydrate Grams	Calories
Round, raw, lean, 4 oz., boneless	0	249
Steak, sirloin, broiled, lean only, 4 oz.	0	235
Steak, T-bone, broiled, lean only, 4 oz.	0	253
°°BEETS, canned, solids & liquid, ½ cup	9.7	42
BLUEFISH, raw, meat only, 4 oz.	0	133
BRAZIL NUTS, shelled, ½ cup (2.5 oz.)	7.6	458
BROCCOLI, frozen, spears, ⅓ pkg.	3.6	26
BROTH, beef, canned, 1 cup	2.6	31
BUTTER, 1 tbl.	0.1	100
CABBAGE, white, raw, 4 oz. weighed untrimmed	4.8	22
CABBAGE, Chinese or celery, raw, sliced, ½ cup	1.1	5
CABBAGE, spoon or bok choy, raw, 4 oz. weighed untrimmed	3.2	17
CANTALOUPE, fresh, ¼ of med.-sized	7.2	29
°°CARAWAY SEEDS, 1 oz.	12.3	72
°°CARROT, raw, 5½″ × 1″	4.8	21
CAULIFLOWER, fresh, raw, 4 oz. weighed untrimmed	2.3	12
CAULIFLOWER, frozen, ⅓ pkg.	3.2	21
CAVIAR, sturgeon, whole eggs, 1 tbl.	0.5	42
CELERY, raw, diced, ½ cup	2.3	10
CELERY, raw, 1 large outer stalk	1.6	7
CHEESE, 1 oz.		
Blue, natural	0.6	104
Cheddar, natural	0.6	113
Cottage, creamed, unflavored	0.8	30
Cream, plain, unwhipped	0.6	106
Edam, natural	0.3	104
Farmer's	0.6	40
Feta, Greek	trace	100
Mozzarella, made from whole milk	0.8	96
Muenster, natural	0.3	100

Food and Quantity	Carbo-hydrate Grams	Calories
Parmesan, natural	0.8	111
Parmesan, natural, grated, 1 tbl.	0.2	31
Pot, uncreamed	0.6	24
Ricotta, Italian style	1.3	50
Roquefort, natural	0.6	104
Swiss Emmenthal, natural, imported	0.5	104
Swiss Gruyère, natural, imported	0.5	104
CHICKEN		
Broiler, cooked, meat only, 4 oz.	0	154
Roaster, cooked, dark meat only, 4 oz.	0	209
Roaster, cooked, light meat only, 4 oz.	0	206
CHICKEN BROTH, canned, 1 cup	0.1	30
°°CHILI SAUCE, 1 tbl.	3.7	16
CHIVES, raw, 1 oz.	1.6	8
°°CHOCOLATE, baking, bitter or unsweetened, 1 oz.	8.2	143
CINNAMON, ground, 1 oz.	25.1	114
CLAM JUICE LIQUOR, bottled or canned, ½ cup	2.5	23
COCOA, dry, unsweetened, Dutch, 1 tbl.	2.9	21
°°CORNSTARCH, 1 teas.	2.3	10
°°CRANBERRIES, fresh, untrimmed, 4 oz.	11.8	50
CREAM, heavy, unwhipped, 1 tbl.	0.5	53
CREAM, sour, 1 tbl.	0.5	25
CUCUMBERS, fresh, eaten without skin, 4 oz. when weighed with skin	2.7	12
CURRY POWDER, 1 teas.	1.3	7
DILL, fresh, probably the same as for PARS-LEY	n.d.a.	n.d.a.
DUCK, raw, domesticated, meat & skin, 4 oz.	0	370
DUCK, raw, domesticated, meat only, 4 oz.	0	187
EGGPLANT, whole, 4 oz. weighed un-trimmed	5.2	23

Food and Quantity	Carbo- hydrate Grams	Calories
EGGS, chicken, raw		
Whole, large	0.4	81
Whole, extra-large	0.5	94
White only, 1, from large egg	0.3	17
Yolk only, 1, from large egg	0.1	59
ENDIVE, Belgian, raw, 4 oz. weighed		
untrimmed	3.2	15
ESCAROLE, raw, 4 oz. weighed untrimmed	4.1	20
FLOUR, soybean, full-fat, 1 oz.	4.4	122
°°FLOUR, wheat, all-purpose, 1 tbl.	6.8	33
GARLIC, raw, peeled, 1 oz.	8.7	39
GELATIN, unflavored, dry, 1 envelope	0	23
GINGER ROOT, fresh, 1 oz. weighed with		
skin	2.5	13
HAM, boiled, canned, 1 oz.	0.3	55
HAM, Italian *prosciutto*	n.d.a.	n.d.a.
JAM, artificially sweetened, Louis Sherry, all		
flavors, 1 jar	3.97	32
JAM, artificially sweetened, all other brands, see		
label on jar		
LAMB, Choice grade, cooked, lean only, leg, 4		
oz.	0	211
LEMON JUICE, fresh, 1 tbl.	1.2	4
LEMON PEEL, fresh, raw, 1 oz.	0.4	n.d.a.
LETTUCE, fresh, 4 oz. weighed untrimmed		
Bibb	2.1	12
Boston	2.1	12
Iceberg	3.3	15
Romaine	2.6	13
LIME JUICE, fresh, 1 tbl.	1.3	4

Food and Quantity	Carbo-hydrate Grams	Calories
LIVER, calf's, raw, 4 oz.	4.7	159
LIVER, chicken, raw, 4 oz.	3.3	146
LOBSTER, raw, 4 oz. weighed whole	0.6	27
LOBSTER, raw, meat only, 4 oz.	0.6	103
MACKEREL, Spanish, raw, meat only	0	201
MARGARINE, 1 tbl.	0.1	101
MAYONNAISE, Hellmann's or Best Foods, 1 tbl.	0.2	97
MINT, fresh	n.d.a.	n.d.a.
MUSHROOMS, fresh, whole, 4 oz. weighed untrimmed	4.9	31
MUSTARD, prepared, brown, 1 teas.	0.5	8
MUSTARD, prepared, Dijon, 1 teas.	0.4	4
OIL, salad or cooking, 1 tbl.		
Olive	0	124
Peanut	0	124
OLIVES,		
Greek style, black, with pits, oil coated, 1 oz.	2.0	77
Green, pitted & drained, 1 oz.	0.4	33
ONIONS, raw		
Whole, 4 oz. weighed untrimmed	9.0	39
Chopped, 1 tbl.	1.0	4
Grated, 1 tbl.	1.2	5
ORANGE PEEL, raw, 1 oz.	7.1	n.d.a.
PARSLEY, fresh, chopped, 1 tbl.	0.3	2
°°PEA PODS, Chinese or edible-podded, snow peas, 4 oz. weighed untrimmed	12.9	57
PECANS, shelled, chopped, 1 tbl.	1.0	48
PEPPER, black, ground, 1 teas.	0.7	4

Food and Quantity	Carbo- hydrate Grams	Calories
PEPPERS, sweet, raw		
Green, whole, 4 oz. weighed untrimmed	4.5	21
Green, chopped, 1 tbl.	0.5	2
Red, whole, 4 oz. weighed untrimmed	6.5	28
PORK, fresh, medium fat, 4 oz.		
All lean cuts, boneless, raw	0	210
Ground, lean only, raw	0	210
Spareribs, raw, with bone	0	244
°°PUMPKIN, canned, ½ cup	9.6	40
°°RASPBERRIES, red, fresh, trimmed, ½ cup	9.8	41
RHUBARB, fresh, 4 oz. weighed untrimmed	1.9	8
ROCK CORNISH HENS	n.d.a.	n.d.a.
	Use figures for CHICKEN	
SALMON, Atlantic, Chinook or king, fresh, raw meat only, 4 oz.	0	250
SALT, table, 1 teas.	0	0
SARDINES, skinless & boneless, canned, 1 can weighing 3¾ oz., canned in olive oil	n.d.a.	341
SAUSAGE, pork, Italian style, cooked, 1 oz.	0.3	86
SCALLIONS, green onions, whole, bulb & entire top, 1 oz.	2.3	10
SHAD, raw, meat only, 4 oz.	0	193
SHALLOTS, raw, 1 oz. weighed with skin	4.2	18
SHRIMP, raw, meat only, 4 oz.	1.7	103
SOLE, raw, fillet, meat only, 4 oz.	0	90
SORREL, sour grass, raw, 4 oz. weighed untrimmed	4.5	22
SOYBEAN CURD (see BEAN CURD, Chinese)		
SOY FLOUR, (see FLOUR, soybean, full-fat)		
SOY SAUCE, all purpose, 1 tbl.	1.4	10

Food and Quantity	Carbo-hydrate Grams	Calories
SPINACH, raw, fresh, 4 oz. weighed untrimmed	3.7	21
SQUASH, SUMMER (see ZUCCHINI)		
STRAWBERRIES, fresh, whole, capped, ½ cup	6.1	27
° °TOMATO SAUCE, canned, plain, ½ cup	8.4	40
TOMATOES, fresh, ripe, whole with skin, 4 oz.	5.3	25
TOMATOES, canned, regular pack, solids & liquid, ½ cup	5.1	25
TUNA FISH, canned in oil, drained solids, 6½ oz. can	0	309
TURNIPS, fresh, white, without tops, raw, 4 oz. weighed with skins	6.4	29
VANILLA, extract, 1 teas.	n.d.a.	8
VEAL, medium fat, raw, boneless, leg, lean meat only, 4 oz.	0	205
VINEGAR, distilled, 1 tbl.	0.8	2
WALNUTS, English or Persian, shelled, chopped, 1 tbl.	1.2	49
° °WATER CHESTNUTS, fresh, raw, whole, 4 oz. weighed unpeeled	16.6	68
WATERCRESS, raw, 4 oz. weighed untrimmed	3.1	20
WATERCRESS, raw, trimmed, ½ cup	0.5	3
° °WORCESTERSHIRE SAUCE, 1 tbl.		
Lea & Perrins	3.0	12
French's	1.4	6
ZUCCHINI, green, fresh, raw, 4 oz. weighed untrimmed	3.9	18

CARBOHYDRATES AND CALORIES
IN SELECTED *LOW-CARBOHYDRATE* FOODS

This is a list of foods that low-carbohydrate dieters should concentrate on. The starred (°°) items are slightly higher in carbohydrates, but are nevertheless good for dieters if used in moderation.

Food and Quantity	Carbo-hydrate Grams	Calories
ABALONE, canned, 4 oz.	2.6	91
ALBACORE, raw, meat only, 4 oz.	0	201
ANCHOVY PASTE, 1 tbl.	1.0	20
APRICOT, fresh, whole, 1 if 12 per pound	4.6	18
ASPARAGUS, fresh, 4 oz. weighed untrimmed	3.2	17
AVOCADO, peeled, pitted		
California variety, ½ cup cubes	4.6	130
Florida variety, ½ cup cubes	6.7	97
BASS, black sea, raw, weighed whole, 1 lb.	0	119
BASS, striped, raw, meat only, 4 oz.	0	165
BEANS, yellow or wax, cooked & drained, 4 oz.	5.2	25
BEEF, chipped, uncooked, ½ cup	0	166
BEET GREENS, fresh, raw whole, 4 oz. weighed untrimmed	2.9	15
°°BLACKBERRIES (including boysenberries, dewberries, and youngberries), fresh, hulled, ½ cup	9.4	42
BLOOD PUDDING or sausage, 1 oz.	0.1	112

Food and Quantity	Carbo-hydrate Grams	Calories
° ° BLUEBERRIES, fresh, trimmed, ½ cup	11.2	45
BOLOGNA, all-meat, 1 oz.	1.0	79
BONITO, raw, meat only, 4 oz.	0	191
BROAD BEANS, Italian, frozen, ⅓ pkg.	4.1	23
BROCCOLI, fresh, raw, whole, 4 oz. weighed untrimmed	4.1	22
° °BRUSSELS SPROUTS, fresh, raw, 4 oz. weighed untrimmed	8.7	47
CABBAGE, spoon, white mustard, or bok choy, fresh, raw, 4 oz. weighed untrimmed	3.2	17
CAPERS, 1 tbl.	1.0	6
CARP, raw, meat only, 4 oz.	0	130
CASABA MELON, fresh, flesh only, 4 oz.	7.4	31
CERVELAT, 1 oz.		
Dry	0.5	128
Soft	0.5	87
CHARD, Swiss, fresh, raw, whole, 4 oz. weighed untrimmed	4.8	26
CHEWING GUM, Bazooka, bubble, sugarless, 1 piece	trace	16
Care Free (Beech Nut), sugarless, 1 stick	trace	6
CHICORY GREENS, fresh, raw, 4 oz. weighed untrimmed	3.5	19
CLAMS, all kinds, raw, meat only, 3 oz.	1.7	65
Canned, meat only, ½ cup	1.5	78
° °COCONUT, fresh, meat only, 4 oz.	10.7	392
° °COCONUT CREAM, liquid expressed from grated coconut, 4 oz.	9.4	379
COCONUT MILK, liquid expressed from a mixture of grated coconut & water, 4 oz.	5.9	286
COD, raw, meat only, 4 oz.	0	88
COLLARD GREENS, fresh, raw, leaves only, 4 oz.	5.8	35

Food and Quantity	Carbo-hydrate Grams	Calories
CONSOMMÉ MADRILÈNE, canned, Crosse & Blackwell, ½ can	2.4	33
CORNED BEEF, cooked, boneless, med. fat, 4 oz.	0	422
CRAB, all species, steamed		
Whole, 4 oz. weighed in shell	0.3	51
Meat only, 1 cup (4.4 oz.)	0.6	116
EGG BEATERS, Fleischmann's, ¼ cup	0.5	100
FENNEL, raw, 4 oz. weighed untrimmed	5.4	30
FILBERTS, shelled, 1 oz.	4.7	180
FLOUNDER, raw, meat only, 4 oz.	0	90
FRANKFURTER, all -beef, 6 oz.	1.1	134
GELATIN DESSERT, dietetic, D-Zerta, all flavors, ½ cup	trace	8
GOOSE, domesticated, roasted, meat & skin, 4 oz.	0	500
°°GRAPEFRUIT, fresh, seedless, pulp only		
White, ½ med. sized (8.5 oz.)	11.9	44
Pink & red, ½ med-sized, (8.5 oz.)	12.8	49
°°GRAPES, Fresh, American type, Concord, Delaware, Niagara, Catawba, & scuppernong, 4 oz. weighed untrimmed	11.2	49
GROUPER, raw, meat only, 4 oz.	0	99
HADDOCK, raw, meat only, 4 oz.	0	90
HAKE, raw, meat only, 4 oz.	0	84
HALIBUT, all varieties, raw, meat only, 4 oz.	0	113
HEADCHEESE, 1 oz.	0.3	76
HERRING, kippered, smoked, 4 oz.	0	239
HICKORY NUTS, shelled, 1 oz.	3.6	191
HONEYDEW MELON, fresh, flesh only, 4 oz.	8.7	37

Food and Quantity	Carbo-hydrate Grams	Calories
HORSERADISH, raw, pared, 1 oz.	5.6	•25
HORSERADISH, prepared, 1 oz.	2.7	11
KALE, raw, leaves only, 4 oz. weighed un-trimmed	6.5	39
KIDNEY, beef, raw, 4 oz.	1.0	147
KIDNEY, lamb, raw, 4 oz.	1.0	119
KINGFISH, raw, meat only, 4 oz.	0	119
KNOCKWURST, all-beef, 1 oz.	0.6	79
KOHLRABI, raw, whole, weighed with skin, without leaves, 4 oz.	5.5	24
LAKE TROUT, raw, meat only, 4 oz.	0	191
°°LITCHI NUTS, fresh, whole, 4 oz. weighed in shell with seeds	11.2	44
LIVER SAUSAGE or LIVERWURST, 1 oz.	0.5	87
MANDARIN ORANGES, canned, unsweetened, solids & liquids, 4 oz.	7.1	31
°°MANGO, fresh, whole, 4 oz. weighed with seeds and skin	12.8	50
MAPLE SYRUP, dietetic (Tillie Lewis), 1 tbl.	0.9	3
°°MILK, dry, nonfat, instant (Carnation), ¼ cup powder	9.4	61
°°MILK, fresh, 1 cup		
Whole, 3.5% fat	12.0	159
Skimmed	12.5	88
Buttermilk, cultured	12.5	88
MORTADELLA, sausage, 1 oz.	0.2	89
MULLET, raw, meat only, 4 oz.	0	166
MUSSELS, Atlantic & Pacific, meat only, 4 oz.	3.7	108
MUSTARD GREENS, raw, whole, 4 oz. weighed untrimmed	4.5	25

Food and Quantity	Carbo-hydrate Grams	Calories
OCEAN PERCH, raw, meat only, 4 oz.	0	108
OCTOPUS, raw, meat only, 4 oz.	0	83
OKRA, raw, whole, 4 oz. weighed untrimmed	7.7	35
OYSTERS, Eastern, meat only, 4 oz.	3.9	75
OYSTERS, Pacific & Western, meat only, 4 oz.	7.3	103
°°PAPAYA, fresh, flesh only, 4 oz.	11.3	44
PÂTÉ DE FOIE GRAS, canned, 1 oz.	1.4	131
°°PEACHES, fresh, whole, 4 oz. weighed unpeeled	9.6	38
PEANUT BUTTER, 1 tbl.		
Skippy, chunk or creamy	2.3	102
Smucker's, creamy or crunchy	2.4	85
Smucker's, old-fashioned	1.6	85
PHEASANT, raw, meat & skin, 4 oz.	0	172
PICKLES, dill, 4″ × 1¾″	3.0	15
PICKLES, cucumber, 4″ × 1¾″	2.7	14
PIKE, raw, meat only, 4 oz.	0	102
PIMENTO, canned, solids & liquids, 1 med.	2.2	10
°°PINEAPPLE, fresh, raw, whole, 4 oz. weighed untrimmed	8.1	31
POLLACK, raw, meat only, 4 oz.	0	108
POMPANO, raw, meat only, 4 oz.	0	188
PORGY, raw, meat only, 4 oz.	0	127
PORK SAUSAGE, all-meat (Jones), 1 oz.	0	n.d.a.
RADISHES, common or Oriental, raw, untrimmed without tops, 4 oz.	3.7	17
RED or GRAY SNAPPER, raw, meat only, 4 oz.	0	105
ROCKFISH, raw, meat only, 4 oz.	0	110
ROE, SHAD, raw, 4 oz.	1.7	147
°°RUTABAGA, raw, diced, ½ cup	7.7	32
SABLEFISH, raw, meat only, 4 oz.	0	215

Food and Quantity	Carbo-hydrate Grams	Calories
SALAMI, all-meat, cooked, 1 oz.	0.4	88
SALAMI, all-meat, dry, 1 oz.	0.3	128
SAND DABS, raw, meat only, 4 oz.	0	90
SALT PORK, without skin, 1 oz.	0	222
TARTAR SAUCE, Hellmann's or Best Foods, 1 tbl.	0.3	73
SAUERKRAUT, canned, drained solids, ½ cup	3.1	16
SCALLOPS, raw, muscle only, 4 oz.	3.7	92
SESAME SEEDS, dry		
Hulled, 1 oz.	5.0	165
Whole, 1 oz.	6.1	160
SESAME SEEDS, liquid, Tahini (A. Sahadi), 1 tbl.	0.8	57
SKATE, raw, meat only, 4 oz.	0	111
SMELTS, all kinds, raw, meat only, 4 oz.	0	111
SNAILS, giant African, 4 oz.	5.0	83
SNAILS, raw, 4 oz.	2.3	102
SOYBEAN MILK, fluid, 4 oz.	2.5	37
SQUAB, pigeon, raw, meat & skin, 4 oz.	0	333
SQUASH, summer, crookneck & straightneck, yellow, fresh, raw, 4 oz. weighed untrimmed	4.8	22
STURGEON, smoked, meat only, 4 oz.	0	169
SWEETBREADS, calf, raw, 4 oz.	0	102
SWORDFISH, raw, meat only, 4 oz.	0	134
°°TANGERINES, whole, 4 oz. weighed untrimmed	9.7	39
TOMATO JUICE, canned, reg. pack, ½ cup	5.2	23
°°TOMATO PASTE, 1 tbl.	3.0	13
TONGUE, beef, med. fat, braised, 4 oz.	0.5	277
TROUT, brook, fresh, raw, meat only, 4 oz.	0	115
TURBOT, Greenland, raw, meat only, 4 oz.	0	166
TURNIP GREENS, fresh, raw, 4 oz. weighed untrimmed	4.8	27

Food and Quantity	Carbo- hydrate Grams	Calories
VEGETABLE JUICE COCKTAIL, canned, 4 oz.	4.1	19
WHITEFISH, lake, raw, meat only, 4 oz.	0	176
YEAST, baker's		
Compressed, 1 oz.	3.1	24
Dry, 1 pkg.	2.7	20
°° YOGURT, unflavored		
Made from whole milk, 1 cup	12.6	122
Made from partially skimmed milk, 8 oz.	11.8	113

CARBOHYDRATES AND CALORIES IN SELECTED *HIGH-CARBOHYDRATE* FOODS

These are foods low-carbohydrate dieters should avoid.

Food and Quantity	Carbo-hydrate Grams	Calories
ANGEL FOOD CAKE, home recipe, 1/12 of 8″ cake	24.1	108
ANGEL FOOD CAKE MIX, prepared as directed, 1/12 of 10″ cake	31.5	137
APPLE, dried, uncooked, ½ cup (1½ oz.)	27.3	106
APPLE, fresh, eaten with skin, 4 oz. weighed untrimmed	15.1	61
APPLE BUTTER, 1 tbl.	8.4	33
APPLE CIDER, ½ cup	14.8	58
APPLE JUICE, canned, ½ cup	14.8	58
APPLE PIE, 2-crust, home recipe, 1/6 of 9″ pie	60.2	404
APPLESAUCE, canned, sweetened with sugar, ½ cup	30.5	116
APPLE TURNOVER, frozen	30.2	315
APRICOTS, canned, sweetened with sugar, heavy syrup, halves & syrup, ½ cup	27.7	108
BAGEL, egg, 3″ dia.	28.0	165
BAGEL, water, 3″ dia.	30.0	165
BANANA PIE, cream or custard, home recipe, 1/6 of 9″ pie	46.7	336
BANANAS, common, fresh, med.-sized, 6.2 oz.	26.4	101

Food and Quantity	Carbo-hydrate Grams	Calories
BARLEY, pearlized, dry, ½ cup	78.8	348
BEANS, baked, 1 cup		
Canned in pork & molasses sauce	53.8	382
Canned with tomato sauce	58.6	306
Canned with pork & tomato sauce	48.4	311
BEANS, kidney or red, dry, 4 oz.	70.2	389
BEANS, lima		
Young, raw, without shell, 4 oz.	25.1	140
Young, cooked, ½ cup	16.8	94
Mature, dry, baby, ½ cup	61.4	331
BEANS, pinto, dry, ½ cup	61.2	335
BEANS, red, Mexican, 4 oz.	72.2	396
BEANS, white, dry, raw, navy or pea, ½ cup	63.8	354
BEEF PIE, home recipe, 4¼" dia., 8 oz. before baking	42.7	558
BISCUIT, baking powder, home recipe, 2" dia., 1 oz. biscuit	12.8	103
BLUEBERRY PIE, home recipe, 2 crust, 1/6 of 9" pie	55.1	382
BOSTON CREAM PIE, home recipe, 1/12 of 8" pie	34.4	208
BRAN FLAKES, raisin, ½ cup	19.8	72
BREAD		
Boston brown, 1.7 oz. slice, 3" × ¾"	21.9	101
Pumpernickel, 0.8 oz. slice, 20 slices per lb.	12.2	57
Raisin, 0.9 oz. slice, 18 slices per lb.	13.4	66
Rye, light, 0.9 oz. slice, 18 slices per lb.	13.0	61
White, enriched or unenriched, 0.8 oz. slice	11.6	62
Whole wheat, prepared with water, 0.9 oz. slice	12.3	60
BREAD CRUMBS, dry, grated, ½ cup	36.7	196
BREADFRUIT, fresh, peeled & trimmed, 4 oz.	29.7	117

Food and Quantity	Carbo-hydrate Grams	Calories
BUCKWHEAT, groats, kasha, 1 oz.	23.3	108
BULGUR, dry, from hard, red, winter wheat, 4 oz.	85.9	401
CANDY [1]		
CASHEW NUTS, ½ cup	20.5	393
CHERRIES		
Sour, canned, pitted, in heavy syrup, ½ cup	29.5	116
Sweet, fresh, whole, 4 oz. weighed with stems	17.8	72
Sweet, canned, pitted, in heavy syrup, 4 oz.	23.2	92
CHERRY PIE, home recipe, 2 crust, 1/6 of 9″ pie	60.7	412
CHESTNUTS, fresh, 4 oz. weighed in shell	38.7	178
CHEWING GUM, sweetened with sugar, 1 stick	2.9	10
CHICK-PEAS or GARBANZOS, dry, ½ cup	61.0	360
CHILI CON CARNE, canned, with beans, 1 cup	30.5	332
CHOCOLATE CAKE, without icing, 3 oz.	44.2	311
CHOCOLATE CAKE, 2 layer, with icing, 1/16 of 10″ cake	67.0	443
CHOCOLATE CHIFFON PIE, home recipe, 1/6 of 9″ pie	61.2	459
CHOCOLATE MERINGUE PIE, home recipe, 1/6 of 9″ pie	46.9	353

[1] Under no circumstances can I advocate eating either candy or cookies when one is dieting. Neither has any nutritional value. However, if you are determined, check Barbara Kraus's *A Dictionary of Calories and Carbohydrates* for a complete listing of brand-name candy and cookies and choose ones with the least carbohydrates. Also, see my sweets recipes in Chapter II of this book.

Food and Quantity	Carbo- hydrate Grams	Calories
CHOCOLATE PUDDING, sweetened with sugar, prepared with milk, ½ cup	29.6	161
CHOCOLATE SYRUP, sweetened with sugar, fudge type, 1 tbl.	10.3	63
CHOCOLATE SYRUP, Hershey's, 1 tbl.	16.7	69
CHUTNEY, 1 tbl.	13.1	53
CITRON, candied, 1 oz.	22.7	89
COCOA MIX, with nonfat dry milk, 1 oz.	20.1	102
COCOA MIX, without nonfat dry milk, 1 oz.	25.3	98
COCONUT, dried, canned or pkg., sweetened, shredded, ½ cup lightly packed	24.5	252
COCONUT CUSTARD PIE, home recipe, 1/6 of 9″ pie	37.8	357
COOKIES [1]		
CORN, fresh, white or yellow, raw, on cob, husk removed, 8 oz.	27.6	120
CORN, fresh, white or yellow, raw, kernels, 4 oz.	25.1	109
CORN, canned, cream style, white or yellow, reg. pkg., ½ cup	25.0	102
CORN FLAKES, cereal, whole, 1 cup (1 oz.)	24.7	112
CORN SYRUP, light or dark blend, 1 tbl.	15.8	61
CORNBREAD, Southern style, home recipe, prepared with whole ground corn meal, 4 oz.	33.0	235
CORNMEAL, white or yellow, dry, degermed, ½ cup	54.1	251
CRACKER MEAL, ½ cup	56.8	352
CRANBERRY SAUCE, canned, sweetened with sugar, strained, ½ cup	51.0	199
CUPCAKE, home recipe, 2¾″ dia., with chocolate icing	29.7	184
CUSTARD APPLE, fresh, flesh only, 4 oz.	28.6	115

Food and Quantity	Carbo- hydrate Grams	Calories
DATES, dry, 4 oz. weighed with pits	71.9	270
DOUGHNUT, cake type, 1 piece (1.1 oz.)	16.4	125
ÉCLAIR, home recipe, custard filling & chocolate		
icing, 4 oz.	26.3	271
FARINA, regular, dry, ½ cup	65.1	314
FIGS, fresh, 4 oz.	23	91
FLOUR		
Carob or St. John's bread, 1 oz.	22.9	51
Chestnut, 1 oz.	21.6	103
Rye, med., 1 oz.	21.2	99
Wheat, all-purpose, 1 oz.	21.6	103
Whole wheat, 1 oz.	20.1	94
FRUIT COCKTAIL, canned, packed in heavy		
syrup, solids & liquid, ½ cup	25.2	97
GELATIN DESSERT, powder, regular, dry, all		
flavors, 3 oz. pkg.	74.8	315
GINGER, candied, 1 oz.	24.7	96
GINGERBREAD, home recipe, 2″ × 2″ ×		
2″	28.6	174
GRAPE JUICE, canned, ½ cup	20.9	83
HONEY, strained, 1 tbl.	16.5	61
ICE CREAM, sweetened with sugar		
10% fat, reg. or French, 1 cup	27.7	257
12% fat, 1 cup	29.3	294
16% fat, rich, 1 cup	26.6	329
Chocolate, Sealtest, ¼ pt.	17.3	136
Vanilla, Lady Borden, 14 % fat, ¼ pt.	17.0	162
Fudge Royale, Sealtest, ¼ pt.	18.2	132
Strawberry, Sealtest, ¼ pt.	19.5	133
ICE MILK, soft-serve, ½ cup	19.6	133

Food and Quantity	Carbo- hydrate Grams	Calories
JAM, sweetened with sugar, 1 tbl.	14.0	54
JELLY, sweetened with sugar, 1 tbl.	12.7	49
JERUSALEM ARTICHOKES, 4 oz. weighed untrimmed	13.1	52
JUJUBE or Chinese dates, fresh, whole, 4 oz. weighed with seeds	29.1	111
KUMQUATS, fresh, 4 oz. weighed with seeds	18.0	69
LEMONADE, frozen concentrate, sweetened with sugar, 6 fl. oz. can	112.0	427
LEMON MERINGUE PIE, home recipe, 1 crust, 1/6 of 9″ pie	52.8	357
LENTILS, whole, dry, 4 oz.	68.2	386
LOGANBERRIES, fresh, 4 oz. weighed with caps	16.1	67
MACARONI, dry, 1 oz.	21.3	105
MALTED MILK MIX, dry, powder, unfortified, 1 oz.	20.1	116
MAPLE SYRUP, 1 tbl.	13.0	50
MARMALADE, sweetened with sugar, 1 tbl.	14.0	51
MATZOS, regular (Manischewitz), 1 matzo	28.1	114
MATZO MEAL (Manischewitz), ½ cup	48.1	219
MILK, CONDENSED, sweetened, canned, 1 cup	166.2	982
MINCE PIE, home recipe, 2 crust. 1/6 of 9″ pie	65.1	428
MOLASSES, Barbados, 1 tbl.	13.3	51
MOLASSES, blackstrap, 1 tbl.	10.4	40
MUFFINS		
Blueberry, home recipe, 3″ muffin (1.4 oz.)	16.8	112
Bran, home recipe, 3″ muffin, (1.4 oz.)	17.2	104

Food and Quantity	Carbo- hydrate Grams	Calories
Corn, home recipe, 3″ muffin (1.4 oz.)	19.2	126
English, Thomas, 1 muffin	28.4	140
NECTARINES, fresh, flesh only, 4 oz.	19.4	73
NOODLES, dry, 1½″ strips, 1 cup	52.6	283
NOODLES, chow mein, canned, 1 cup	26.1	220
OATMEAL, regular, dry, ½ cup	24.6	141
ORANGES, fresh, whole, med. sized, 3″ dia. (5.5 oz.)	19.0	77
ORANGE PEEL, candied, 1 oz.	22.9	90
PANCAKES, home recipe, wheat 1 4″ pancake	9.2	62
PASTINAS, dry, egg, 1 oz.	20.4	109
PEAS, mature seeds, dry, split, without seedcoat, ½ cup	63.7	353
PEA SOUP, canned, green, prepared with equal volume of water, 1 cup	22.5	130
PEARS, fresh, whole, 4 oz. weighed untrimmed	15.8	63
PICKLES, cucumber, bread & butter, ½ cup	15.2	62
PICKLES, cucumber, sweet, whole, 1 oz.	10.3	41
PIE CRUST, home recipe, baked for 9″ pie, 1 crust	78.8	900
PINEAPPLE JUICE, canned, unsweetened, ½ cup	16.7	68
PIZZA, frozen, baked, ⅛ of 14″ pie	26.6	184
PLANTAINS, raw, flesh only, 4 oz.	35.4	135
PLUMS, Damson, fresh, whole, 4 oz. weighed with pits	18.4	68
POTATO CHIPS, 1 oz.	21.5	111
POTATO SALAD, home recipe, made with mayonnaise, hard-cooked egg and seasonings, ½ cup	16.8	181

Food and Quantity	Carbo-hydrate Grams	Calories
POTATOES, raw, whole, 4 oz. weighed un-pared	15.7	70
POTATOES, french-fried in deep fat, 10 pieces, each 2″ × ½″ × ½″	20.5	156
PRETZELS, 1 oz.	21.5	111
PRUNES, dried, "softenized," uncooked, med.-sized, whole, with pits, ½ cup	53.6	203
PRUNES, canned, stewed, pitted (Del Monte), ½ cup	37.5	144
PRUNE JUICE, ½ cup	24.3	99
PUMPKIN PIE, home recipe, 1 crust, 1/6 of 9″ pie	37.2	321
RAISINS, dried, whole, 4 oz.	87.8	328
RICE		
Brown, cooked, 4 oz.	28.9	135
White, regular, raw, ½ cup	79.6	359
White, regular, cooked, ½ cup	24.7	111
SHERBET, orange, ½ cup	29.7	130
SODA, sweetened with sugar, all flavors [2]		
SPAGHETTI, dry, 1 oz.	21.3	105
SPONGE CAKE, home recipe, 1/12 of 10″ cake	35.7	196
SQUASH, Butternut, baked, flesh only, 4 oz.	19.8	77
SUCCOTASH, frozen, cooked, drained, ½ cup	19.7	89
SUGAR		
Brown, 1 tbl.	12.5	48
Confectioner's, 1 tbl. unsifted	7.7	30
Granulated, 1 tbl.	11.9	46

[2] All soda sweetened with sugar is much too high in carbohydrates for any dieter to use. Six ounces of the average sugar-sweetened soda contain approximately 20 grams of carbohydrates and approximately 80 calories—neither of which have any nutritional value.

Food and Quantity	Carbo-hydrate Grams	Calories
SWEET POTATOES, raw, all kinds, 4 oz. weighed with skin	24.2	105
TAPIOCA, dry, quick-cooking, granulated, ¼ cup	32.8	134
WAFFLES, home recipe, 7″ dia. (2.6 oz.)	28.1	209
WATERMELON, fresh, wedge, 2 lbs., 4″ × 8″ with rind	27.3	111
YAMS, raw, 4 oz. weighed with skin	22.6	99
YOGURT [3]		

[3] All flavored yogurt, no matter which brand or flavor, is high in carbohydrates and should be avoided.

CARBOHYDRATES AND CALORIES IN WINES AND OTHER ALCOHOLIC BEVERAGES

Even though these charts are accurate as far as literal carbohydrate and calorie values are concerned, they do not and cannot take into account the effect of alcohol on the body.

Alcohol makes the body produce insulin. Since one of the normal functions of insulin is to convert carbohydrates into fat, anything that increases the insulin level will fatten you faster. At the same time, the effect of alcohol varies from one individual to another. So, despite the fact that literal carbohydrate values are shown here, a dieter should experiment and adjust his alcoholic intake according to what it does to him in particular. No hard and fast rules can be drawn.

Assorted Alcoholic Beverages

Food and Quantity	Carbo-hydrate Grams	Calories
ANISETTE		
Garnier, 54 proof, 1 oz.	9.3	82
Old Mr. Boston, 60 proof, 1 oz.	7.5	90
B & B LIQUEUR, 86 proof, 1 fl. oz.	5.7	94
BEER		
Regular, 4.5% alcohol, 12 fl. oz.	13.7	151
Lo Carbo Dia Beer, 12 fl. oz.	4.2	145
BITTER LEMON, 6 fl. oz.	23.6	96
BITTER ORANGE, 6 fl. oz.	22.6	92
BITTERS, Angostura, 1 fl. oz.	12.5	86

Food and Quantity	Carbo- hydrate Grams	Calories
CHERRY HEERING, liqueur (Hiram Walker), 49		
proof, 1 fl. oz.	10.0	80
CHERRIES, MARASCHINO, 1 average cherry	1.9	8
CRÈME DE CASSIS LIQUEUR, Garnier, 60 proof,		
1 fl. oz.	13.5	83
CURAÇAO LIQUEUR, Garnier, 60 proof, 1 fl.		
oz.	12.7	100
DAIQUIRI COCKTAIL		
Liquid mix, Party Tyme, 2 fl. oz.	19.4	81
Liquid mix, Party Tyme, banana, 2 fl. oz.	14.6	59
DISTILLED LIQUOR, unflavored bourbon whis-		
key, brandy, Canadian whiskey, gin, Irish		
whisky, rum, rye whisky, Scotch whisky,		
tequila, and vodka		
80 proof, 1 fl. oz.	trace	65
86 proof, 1 fl. oz.	trace	70
90 proof, 1 fl. oz.	trace	74
94 proof, 1 fl. oz.	trace	77
100 proof, 1 fl. oz.	trace	83
DRAMBUIE LIQUEUR, 80 proof, Hiram Walker, 1		
fl. oz.	11.0	110
GIN, sloe, Garnier, 60 proof, 1 fl. oz.	8.5	83
KIRSCHWASSER, Leroux, 96 proof, 1 fl. oz.	0	80
MANHATTAN COCKTAIL, Hiram Walker, 55		
proof, 3 fl. oz.	3.0	147
MARTINI COCKTAIL		
Gin, Hiram Walker, 67.5 proof, 3 fl. oz.	0.6	168
Vodka, Hiram Walker, 60 proof, 3 fl. oz.	0	147
OLD-FASHIONED, Hiram Walker, 62 proof,		
3 fl. oz.	3.0	165

Food and Quantity	Carbo- hydrate Grams	Calories
PINA COLADA, Party Tyme, canned, 12½% alcohol, 2 fl. oz.	5.1	63
QUININE TONIC WATER, sweetened with sugar		
Canada Dry, 6 fl. oz.	17.6	68
Schweppes, 6 fl. oz.	16.5	66
QUININE TONIC WATER, artificially sweetened, dietetic No-Cal, 6 fl. oz.	0	2
TIA MARIA, liqueur, Hiram Walker, 63 proof, 1 fl. oz.	10.0	92
TOM COLLINS, canned, Party Tyme, 10% alcohol, 2 fl. oz.	5.9	58
TOM COLLINS MIXER SOFT DRINK		
Canada Dry, 6 fl. oz.	15.0	61
Hoffman, 6 fl. oz.	16.1	64
TRIPLE SEC LIQUEUR, Garnier, 60 proof, 1 fl. oz.	8.5	83
VERMOUTH, dry & extra dry, Noilly Prat, 16% alcohol 3 fl. oz.	1.6	101
VERMOUTH, sweet, Noilly Prat, 16% alcohol, 3 fl. oz.	12.1	128
VODKA SCREWDRIVER, Old Mr. Boston, 25 proof, 3 fl. oz.	10.5	117
WHISKEY SOUR, canned, Hiram Walker, 3 fl. oz.	12.0	177

Wines

BEAUJOLAIS, French, Burgundy		
Barton & Guestier, St. Louis, 12% alcohol, 3 fl. oz.	0.1	60

Food and Quantity	Carbo- hydrate Grams	Calories
Chanson, St. Vincent, 11% alcohol, 3 fl.		•
oz.	6.3	84
BURGUNDY		
Gallo, 13% alcohol, 3 fl. oz.	0.9	52
Louis M. Martini, 12½% alcohol, 3 fl. oz.	0.2	90
BURGUNDY, SPARKLING		
Barton & Guestier, French red, 12% alcohol, 3		
fl. oz.	2.2	69
Chanson, French red, 3 fl. oz.	3.6	72
Taylor, 12½% alcohol, 3 fl. oz.	1.8	78
CHABLIS		
Barton & Guestier, 12% alcohol, 3 fl. oz.	0.1	60
Chanson, St. Vincent, 11½% alcohol, 3 fl.		
oz.	6.3	81
Gallo, 12% alcohol, 3 fl. oz.	0.9	50
Louis M. Martini, 12½% alcohol, 3 fl. oz.	0.2	90
CHAMPAGNE		
Bollinger, 3 fl. oz.	3.6	72
Mumm's Cordon Rouge, brut, 12%, 3 fl.		
oz.	1.4	65
Veuve Cliquot, 12½% alcohol, 3 fl. oz.	0.6	78
CHATEÂUNEUF-DU-PAPE		
Barton & Guestier, 13½% alcohol,		
3 fl. oz.	0.5	70
Chanson, 13% alcohol, 3 fl. oz.	6.3	90
CHIANTI		
Antinori, Classico, 12½% alcohol, 3 fl. oz.	6.3	87
Brolio Classico, 13% alcohol, 3 fl. oz.	0.3	66
CLARET		
Gold Seal, 12% alcohol, 3 fl. oz.	0.4	82
COLD DUCK		
Italian Swiss Colony—Private Stock, 12½% al-		
cohol, 3 fl. oz.	4.3	75
CONCORD WINE		
Mogen David, 12% alcohol, 3 fl. oz.	16.0	120

Food and Quantity	Carbo-hydrate Grams	Calories
GEWÜRZTRAMINER		
Willm Alsatian, 11–14% alcohol, 3 fl. oz.	3.6	66
MADEIRA		
Leacock, 19% alcohol, 3 fl. oz.	6.3	120
MARGAUX, French red Bordeaux		
Barton & Guestier, 12% alcohol, 3 fl. oz.	0.4	62
MARSALA		
Italian Swiss Colony—Private Stock, 19.7% alcohol, 3 fl. oz.	7.1	124
PINOT CHARDONNAY		
Louis M. Martini, 12½% alcohol, 3 fl. oz.	0.2	90
PORT		
Gallo, ruby, 20% alcohol, 3 fl. oz.	8.8	112
Robertson, ruby, 20% alcohol, 3 fl. oz.	9.9	138
Robertson, tawny, 21% alcohol, 3 fl. oz.	9.9	145
POUILLY-FUISSÉ, French white Burgundy		
Barton & Guestier, 12½% alcohol, 3 fl. oz.	0.3	64
Chanson, St. Vincent, 12% alcohol, 3 fl. oz.	6.3	84
POUILLY-FUMÉ, French white, Loire Valley		
Barton & Guestier, 12% alcohol, 3 fl. oz.	0.1	60
RIESLING, Alsatian		
Willm, 11–14% alcohol, 3 fl. oz.	3.6	66
ROSÉ		
Chanson Rosé des Anges, 12% alcohol, 3 fl. oz.	6.3	84
Nectarose, Vin Rosé d'Anjou, 12% alcohol, 3 fl. oz.	2.6	70
ROSÉ, SPARKLING		
Chanson, 3 fl. oz.	3.6	72
SAINT-ÉMILION, French Bordeaux		
Barton & Guestier, 12% alcohol, 3 fl. oz.	0.7	63
SAUTERNES, French white Bordeaux		
Barton & Guestier, 13% alcohol, 3 fl. oz.	7.6	95
SHERRY, CREAM		
Gallo, 20% alcohol, 3 fl. oz.	8.3	111

Food and Quantity	Carbo- hydrate Grams	Calories
Williams & Humbert, Canasta, 20½% alcohol, 3 fl. oz.	5.4	150
SHERRY, DRY		
Dry Sack, Williams & Humbert, 20½% alcohol, 3 fl. oz.	4.5	120
Gallo, 20% alcohol, 3 fl. oz.	1.7	84
SHERRY, MEDIUM		
Italian Swiss Colony—Private Label, 19.8% al- cohol, 3 fl. oz.	2.8	108
Taylor, 19½% alcohol, 3 fl. oz.	7.1	132
SOAVE, Italian white		
Antinori, 12% alcohol, 3 fl. oz.	6.3	84
SYLVANER		
Louis M. Martini, 12½% alcohol, 3 fl. oz.	0.2	90
VALPOLICELLA, Italian red		
Antinori, 3 fl. oz.	6.3	84

Index